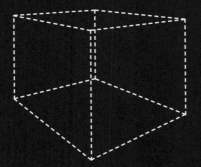

THE ETHICAL ARCHITECT

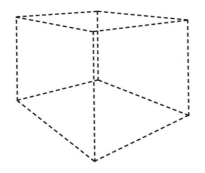

THE ETHICAL ARCHITECT
the dilemma of contemporary practice

tom spector

PRINCETON ARCHITECTURAL PRESS
NEW YORK

For Susan and for Hugh and with the deepest gratitude
to Sam and Virginia Spector

published by
Princeton Architectural Press
37 East Seventh Street
New York, New York 10003

For a free catalog of books, call 1.800.722.6657.
Visit our web site at www.papress.com.

Project editing: Clare Jacobson
Text editing: Nancy Eklund Later
Design: David Konopka

Special thanks to:
Nettie Aljian, Ann Alter, Amanda Atkins, Jan Cigliano,
Jane Garvie, Mark Lamster, Anne Nitschke, Lottchen
Shivers, Jennifer Thompson, and Deb Wood of Princeton
Architectural Press —Kevin C. Lippert, publisher

Library of Congress Cataloging-in-Publication Data
Spector, Tom, 1957-
    The ethical architect : the dilemma of contemporary
practice / Tom Spector.
        p. cm.
    Includes bibliographical references and index.
    ISBN 1-56898-284-4 (hardcover : alk. paper)—
ISBN 1-56898-285-2 (paperback : alk. paper)
    1. Architects—Professional ethics. 2. Architecture—
Moral and ethical aspects.   I. Title.
    NA1995 .S68 2001
    174'.972--dc21
                                        2001002302

CONTENTS

ACKNOWLEDGMENTS This book owes much to the generous access and support given me by the faculty in the Department of Philosophy at the University of California, Berkeley. In particular, chapter one derived much of its impetus from the guidance (and forbearance) of Samuel Scheffler and chapter six benefited similarly from that of Richard Wollheim. Much to my good fortune, Bernard Williams, whose father was an architect, agreed to be on my dissertation committee. The work on that project formed the basis of this book. Professor Williams was especially helpful in guiding me through some of the roughest spots of chapter four. Many thanks are also due for the support and perseverance of the members of my committee from the College of Architecture at Berkeley: W. Mike Martin, Jean-Pierre Protzen, and my chairman, Stephen Tobriner. In particular, Professor Protzen's comments on chapter three helped correct the worst of its omissions and chapter five would not have been possible without Professor Tobriner's depth on the subject of seismic design. Furthermore, it was a suggestion of Professor Tobriner's that led to the overall organization of this inquiry around the Vitruvian values of utilitas, firmitas, and venustas. The participation of the Structural Engineers' Association of Northern California and the comments and perspectives contributed by Bret Lizundia, Charles Bloszies, and Nick Forell were crucial for the development of chapter 5.

Finally, I would like to thank Clare Jacobson and Nancy Eklund Later at the Princeton Architectural Press for their commitment to this project during the past year. The book was enhanced immeasurably by their careful editing and enthusiastic guidance.

THE ETHICAL ARCHITECT

Architecture's moral mission reached the nadir of its decline in the 1970s, after the critiques of modernism formulated by Jane Jacobs and Robert Venturi unleashed a thoroughgoing repudiation of the movement's moral pretensions. The revolutionary ideal of solving societal problems through design that was so vehemently proclaimed by modernism's proponents in the heroic age of the 1930s was exposed as hollow, and the architecture profession fell into a state of ethical disarray. In 1979, when the mandatory code of ethics of the American Institute of Architects (AIA) was withdrawn under threat of anti-trust action by the Justice Department, the profession seemed little more than a self-serving business venture. Architecture's failure to address the real problems faced by users of the built environment, as perceived from within and without, left its core design values in shambles.

By 1987, the AIA had managed to craft a new code of ethics that more closely resembled a statement of values than a monopolistic restraint of trade, but the postmodern critique of modern architecture's shortcomings had further eroded consensus on architecture's central design values. Other critics joined the fray: social scientists questioned the legitimacy of professional morality; feminists and minorities articulated architecture's many unspoken coercions; disability-rights activists successfully portrayed the existing conditions of the built environment as an evil to be legislated against. Given such demoralizing circumstances, the esoteric doctrine of deconstruction easily gained a toehold, with its denial of any connection at all between design and moral value. Rather than quell architects' sense of moral unease, however, this development only served to fracture still further the idea that architectural design could coalesce around a core mission or statement of purpose.

Architects live and work today in a functioning but weakened profession that lacks a dominant design ethic. Views regarding the desirability of this development within the field span the gamut, from "good riddance to unwanted baggage" to a nostalgic desire to recapture the sense of purpose and idealism with which the masters of modernism and their champions swept the world off its feet. An opportunity to examine unquestioned assumptions regarding the morality of professional practice and the value of design has emerged. The past can be mined both for its good ideas and for its bad examples, and a future of possible convergence upon a durable, substantial, and robust design ethic can be imagined.

A conversation about the content of a design ethic reflective of architecture's core values has persisted. For the most part, this dialogue could be characterized as an effort to exhort the architectural troops to redouble their efforts in maintaining the highest level of professionalism, renewing the commitment to serve, and working to make really good buildings. The trouble with this approach is that abuse of professional status, lack of service orientation, and a diminished commitment to quality design are not what brought architecture to this point in the first place. The profession's ethical disarray may be more accurately described as the result of vague and unsustainable promises to society and of an unnecessarily narrow view of what constitutes an ethical outlook brought on by modernism's exclusive reliance on a philosophy of utilitarianism. No redoubling of efforts will fix these problems. A strong sense of commitment, though laudable, is of little effect without a clearly articulated concept of a moral mission.

Architects need not assume that they are on their own in the project of articulating a strong ethic of practice. A distinguished body of thought dedicated to discussing these kinds of problems is at hand in the form of moral philosophy. The purpose of this book is to add to and enlarge this fledgling conversation by bringing in ideas and arguments developed by this heretofore ignored source of guidance.

Moral philosophy has been left out of the currents of architectural discourse for several reasons. First, even in the wake of modernism's decline, the movement's claim to have solved the ethical problem by embracing the utilitarian doctrine of functionalism has cast a long shadow on contemporary architectural thinking. Second, moral philosophy's long tradition reaching back to Plato has been overshadowed as well by other philosophical movements. Exciting and revolutionary movements of the twentieth century, such as logical positivism, Marxism, linguistic analysis, structuralism, and deconstruction, have captured the contemporary imagination in ways that the more staid investigations of moral philosophy could not. In fairness, moral philosophy has shown little interest in architecture either. With only a few notable exceptions, moral philosophers have been generally content to converse with other moral philosophers and let others outside the discipline decide for themselves whether their conversations have any relevance or applicability. This lack of interdisciplinary cross-pollination is a shame, because moral philosophy, which has grown noticeably more vibrant and diverse in recent times, has much to offer.

The project here, then, is not to introduce architects to the rudiments of moral philosophy but rather to take advantage of the fact that moral philosophy has preceded us down many of the avenues of thought that could be fruitfully pursued in an ongoing effort to bring a sense of unified purpose back to architecture. Such a project can only start where the exhausted ones left off: with an examination of the embattled professional agenda and of the fragmented concept of what constitutes good design. Architects may well have lost the messianic zeal of early modernism for good, but the prospects for reacquainting architecture and morality in the hopes of establishing a more companionable, if perhaps less glamorous, relationship are good.

CHAPTER 1 | PRACTICE

An architectural scandal rocked my hometown of Rome, Georgia, in the early 1990s. The brouhaha started when roof leaks developed under the false dormers on Floyd County's brand new, neo-traditional airport terminal. These were not mere spot leaks in the ceiling that could be stopped with a careful caulking job; they were buckets-on-the-floor leaks, the possible cause of which quickly became a favorite topic of conversation in doughnut shops across three counties. Theories of who was to blame quickly developed. The embarrassed Airport Commission faulted the general contractor; the contractor, in turn, pointed the finger of blame at the metal roof sub-contractor; and the roofer identified the architect as the party responsible for the leaks. The county attorney—who considered himself something of a roofing expert in light of the fact that his family owned a roofing business—declared the problem hopeless and announced that the entire standing-seam roof would have to be torn off and replaced.

The chief building inspector bravely waded in to the fray to identify the source of the problem. While reviewing the project drawings, he noticed something far more interesting than a poor flashing detail. The only stamped drawings contained in the building set were the engineer's. The architect's stamp was nowhere in evidence. Upon further investigation, the building inspector discovered that the man who had contracted with the county to prepare the drawings—let's call him Bill—was not licensed to practice architecture in the state of Georgia.

Bill had, in fact, been practicing in the area for several years before his secret caught up with him. He tried to explain to the Airport Commission that his lack of licensing in Georgia was simply the result of a bureaucratic reciprocity issue with an adjacent state, where he actually *was* licensed, but no one listened. The story occupied the front page of the *Rome News-Tribune* for two weeks and led to a predictable progression of events.[1] Bill was investigated, convicted of a misdemeanor, and forbidden from ever practicing architecture in Georgia again. His career is most likely ruined.

I followed Bill's story with horror and satisfaction: horror, as Bill's career was devoured with all the spectacle of my hometown's namesake city, and satisfaction, as the county government's discomfort mounted. The indignant wail of a county commission that suddenly thought it had been duped out of its design fee by an impostor was solid gold. Why, I wondered, was the group that was so proud of its stately, though slightly soggy, airport terminal one day outraged about it the next? The building was still the same. It even turned out that the leaks in the roof were not the architect's fault; the dormers had not been installed as drawn, and reinstallation eventually solved the majority of problems. The county commissioners, however, were still not satisfied. They wanted something from their architect beyond a mere commodity.

Bill would have to pay for his infraction. It was clearly fraudulent for him to have assumed the benefits of being a professional architect without having passed the exam or pledged his commitment to uphold state law. He wanted those benefits without paying the price, and this created an untenable situation. There is more to be said about Bill's fraudulent activities than this, however. Bill had violated the

4

public trust. As a result, the County Airport Commission felt cheated, leading one commissioner to go so far as to suggest that Bill pay all expenses related to the roof's repair.[2]

As the controversy surrounding Bill's transgression illustrates, fulfilling one's professional obligations as an architect entails not only the skillful application of a certain type of knowledge but adherence to certain ethical standards as well. Turning one's back on professional obligations is a serious and ugly thing. In having done so, Bill is not alone. Between 1997 and 1999, California issued twenty-two convictions or enforcement actions against individuals for practicing without a license. In 1999, a bribery scandal involving architects, interior designers, contractors, and client representatives was exposed in New York City, resulting in thirty-one criminal prosecutions. Although the desire to ignore such transgressions is understandable, unless one is willing to recognize that the concept of professionalism encompasses not only ideals but also boundaries, then professional morality cannot be said to have demonstrable content.

THE PROFESSIONAL OBLIGATIONS OF AN ARCHITECT

The role of the architect involves obligations that are not easily reduced to issues of mere technical competence. An architect addresses clients' needs through the medium of the built environment and helps protect the public against the dangers of shoddy and insensitive building. In assuming these obligations, an architect is charged with resolving often incommensurate demands. It is this activity, ultimately, that justifies the architect's special status as a professional and distinguishes him or her from, say, an artist or technician. The architect is hired, at least in part, to take on the ethical dilemmas of building. By mediating between private and public

5

demands, for instance, or by weighing the risks of technological innovation against those of stagnation, an architect puts his or her professional status on the line. Bill violated his professional obligation by pretending, not that he possessed sufficient technical skill to do the job (which he was ultimately shown to have had), but that he was sitting on this moral hot-seat when, in fact, he was not. Like discovering that your insurance agent had pocketed your premium after your policy expires, you feel cheated, even if you made no claims, because you realize that no one had been sharing the risk with you.

In addition to deliberating over dilemmatic issues, professional architects assume a variety of moral obligations; they make various promises that can only be reneged on without penalty under extreme circumstances. They agree to abide by registration laws that are quite explicit, both on matters of their conduct and on the sorts of protections they are to provide the public. In addition, both state registration and membership in the American Institute of Architects (AIA) depend upon the architect's recognition of certain "negative" duties. In some states, these duties include never having been convicted of a crime involving moral turpitude.[3] While there is probably much that is self-serving in such regulations, the public may have a legitimate right to expect that the architect in whom it places a considerable amount of trust is not a known extortionist, murderer, or drug dealer. Along with adequate knowledge and demonstrable skill, society values high moral character in its professionals.

As suggested above, the architect's obligations arise from and respond to two sets of needs. Individual members of society require someone to construct buildings that presumably accord with their needs, and the public at large requires someone to protect it from the potentially devastating effects of poor and insensitive building practices.

Although assisted by local building departments and others, only the architect is allowed to address these needs in total and is actually forbidden to address them in piecemeal fashion. The dual nature of the architect's role distinguishes it from that of other professionals. Imagine how the legal landscape would look, for instance, if attorneys were required to certify that all of their briefs and motions were aimed at the public's protection, as well as their client's.

An architect's identification with his or her role serves to motivate and guide the professional's actions and to establish a set of expectations on the part of the public. Architects are compelled to consider design strategies or building solutions beyond their own or their client's egoistic wishes in a fair, responsible, well-meaning, and non-cynical way. Society has the right to expect that an architect will give full consideration to the moral dilemmas of building. Negotiating a balance between legitimate public concerns and private demands is at the heart of the architect's professional obligation. Society can be sure it is receiving such consideration only if an architect puts his right to fulfill these professional obligations on the line each time he or she practices. The architect's stamp on a set of drawings is evidence that such consideration has been given.

PROFESSIONAL MORALITY

The fact that Bill never stamped his drawings does not preclude the possibility that he gave conscientious consideration to the ethical issues involved in the airport terminal's design. Indeed, during the airport fiasco, Bill comported himself somewhat honorably; despite the drubbing he took from all quarters, he stayed on the project and helped solve its problems. But Bill's actions may be condemned on another level, through a consideration of professional morality.

A profession is often said to combine the skillful application of technical knowledge with an ethic of practice.[4] Although the content of the knowledge base differs from profession to profession, it is both highly specialized and sufficiently broad to allow the professional to choose among alternative courses of action. A high degree of competence is required to choose wisely. The knowledge base of medical and legal professionals fits well within these constraints, as does that of most architectural professionals.

Determining the content of a professional code of ethics poses a different sort of problem. Professional ethics guide and constrain the actions of professionals in ways that diverge from ordinary or everyday morality. This brings up the probability of conflict between the values of the professional and those of society at large. How professional ethics might differ from those of society in general, and why society might give special protections to a group of people who possess a different set of values, forms the subject of Bernard Williams' essay, "Professional Morality and its Dispositions." Williams identifies a number of possible explanations for society's willingness to accept the divergence between professional and societal morality. The most plausible explanation is contained in Williams' concept of the "uneasy professional." The professional, according to this concept, feels compelled to reconcile societal values with his professional norms. This need for reconciliation creates inner conflict. The "uneasy professional" continually looks for ways to reduce this conflict. Society benefits from this, in that it prevents the professional from becoming complacent about his or her professional tasks. Living with a certain amount of internal conflict is the price professionals pay in exchange for special status, regulated entry into the field, and some degree of business monopoly.[5]

8

Society also benefits from this arrangement by being able to entrust a group of people with shouldering some of its more difficult ethical dilemmas. In the case of lawyers, for instance, society passes off the responsibility of reconciling the rights of the accused with its own. In the case of professional architects, society benefits by handing over the responsibility of reconciling private and public rights within the built environment to someone who possesses expertise and goodwill toward both sides. Architect Henry Cobb provides evidence of Williams' theory of the "uneasy professional" when he states,

> I cannot recall a single commission undertaken by my firm in the past thirty years that has not required us to make difficult choices concerning how and to whom we render our professional service and how and to whom the intended building will make itself useful. These choices are difficult because the numerous constituencies whom we, as a matter of professional responsibility, see ourselves as serving—the client institution, the building's users, its neighbors, and so on—these diverse constituencies are often fiercely committed to widely divergent and deeply conflicting principles of human duty . . . Hence, a disquieting ambivalence with respect to ethical issues—a pervasive uncertainty about how best to fulfill my duty as a professional—is a nearly perpetual state of mind for me, as surely it must also be for every architect in practice today whose work significantly touches or shapes the public realm.[6]

What challenge does the concept of the "uneasy professional" present to someone who would act fraudulently? In addition to possessing technical knowledge and engaging in conscientious deliberations over the most dilemmatic problems, the "uneasy professional" also attempts to reconcile his professional values with those of the general public with goodwill toward both.

9

The fraud claims to give consideration to important dilemmas, but against what value system? He cannot share the profession's values—values he deliberately set out to circumvent. To the degree to which he is willing to deceive, he cannot claim to feel strongly about society's values either. Any deliberations he engages in cannot be carried out in the personal way in which the "uneasy professional" could— the way in which society stands to benefit most. A fraud cannot bridge the gap between what he is and what he pretends to be.

Willingness to recognize the importance of character and to embrace one's uneasy position is only the first step, however, toward re-establishing architecture's moral mission and securing a defensible role for architecture in the world at large. Other writers on the subject of architectural practice have argued that the profession must be substantially remodeled for these goals to be achieved.

CONTRACTARIAN AND CONFLICT THEORIES

The notion that architects engage in an ethically significant contract with society derives from the application of ideas developed in earlier times and in other disciplines to the profession of architecture. Contractarian thought has its origins in the seventeenth century and the writings of the English philosopher Thomas Hobbes. In his *Leviathan*, Hobbes outlines the concept of the social contract, describing the voluntary "failing of performance" as a "Violation of Faith."[7] Finding Hobbes' view that contracts derive their value from the restrictions they place on participants unnecessarily pessimistic, contemporary philosophers John Rawls and David Gauthier have attempted to revise contractarian theory in the twentieth century to emphasize the gains resulting from cooperation.[8] This idea of society as a "cooperative venture for mutual advantage"[9] recognizes the legitimate societal benefits to be had from specialization and from delegating authority to those best able to exercise it in their areas of expertise. In such a mutual benefit model, the promises and obligations made by each party, on which the other will rely, contain an ethical component. One need not hold that the contractarian idea is the only source of moral obligation to embrace this position, only that the implicit contract is part of the equation. In the unique activity we call the professional practice of architecture, however, the idea of a contract is central.[10]

Some observers would argue, however, that the relationship between the professionals and society is better understood in terms of power relations, rather than ethics. Magali Larson and other social scientists looking at the professions argue, in effect, that no form of a contract actually exists between the professional and society.[11]

For Larson and other proponents of conflict theory, the story of professionalization is primarily one of an occupational group asserting itself for its own gain.[12] Professionalization is seen as little more than a process of self-aggrandizement, whereby a group of would-be professionals organize, set norms of practice, legitimize their knowledge base by making it part of an academic curriculum, devise a means of controlling entry into the occupation, secure governmental approval of their restrictive practices, and demand public recognition of their professional status, thereby establishing their turf and protecting it against encroachment by other, would-be professionals. This often repeated theory of professional-ization has become commonplace within the sociology of the professions.

Larson's approach effectively denies the relevance of any discussion of the moral aspects of professionalization.[13] To

11

elbow one's way to the top of society's heap and then talk about one's ethics would produce only self-serving rhetoric. No wonder architects experience inner conflict; that conflict derives from a desire to do the morally good thing in the face of one's own obvious egoism, manifest in the struggle for professionalization.

Dana Cuff's exposition on current architectural practice tends to reinforce this theory of professionalization by picturing a coercive group of professionals constantly trying to convince all comers of the preferability of the architect's artistic vision.[14] This scenario may be incomplete in critical ways. Sociologist David Brain maintains, for example, that no group short of the military is strong enough to assert itself in the way described by conflict theorists, unless it piggybacks on the structures of work and remuneration that were developed prior to professionalization.[15] Historian of the professions Bruce Kimball takes this argument a step further by showing that the professions are not so much ideologically based as they are historically based, the structure of professionalism closely interwoven with the history of society. He maintains that the "true professional ideal" emerged only in the twentieth century, in response to changing societal circumstances not accounted for by conflict theorists.[16] If Kimball's thesis is true and the establishment of the architectural professions, as well as other professions, grew organically out of the development of society, then there is good reason to think of the professions as grounded in an ever-renewed bargain with society.[17]

One could also question whether the conclusions supported by conflict theory resonate with the self-perception of architects. There is no evidence to support that architects experience inner conflict over their own egotistical struggles for power. Architects' inner conflict tends to focus on how best to promote the beauty of the built environment in the face of the an-aesthetic values of capitalism, or how to represent the interests of groups that are not

12

present during design, or how to bring meaning to desultory suburban landscapes. What architects are not in a dilemma about is how to reconcile their moral feelings with their achievement of a coercive monopoly over a segment of the building industry.[18]

THE DIMINISHED ARCHITECT

Subscribing to the outlook of conflict theory makes advocating substantial changes to the structure of architectural practice seems less traumatic than it would to a contractarian. To a conflict theorist, the assertion of professionalism was a unilateral move and it can just as easily be undone unilaterally. It is for this reason unsurprising that the suggestion that architects improve their lot by becoming something more akin to an expert consultant than a concerned professional would come from this camp. In an effort to reduce inner conflict, architects could shed their obligations to the public and concentrate simply on designing beautiful things.

What would be gained by such a restructuring of the architectural profession? Architecture would no longer be vulnerable to the approbation suffered at the hands of frauds such as Bill, because the fundamentals of goodwill would no longer be at issue, only the artistic merits of a design. The need for someone involved in the building process to take on the role of guardian of the public interest would be met by other means. Perhaps owners would be held liable for a building's meeting safety codes and for making sure that their design consultants did their job properly. Or perhaps building inspection departments would be beefed up to provide design monitoring as well as in-depth construction supervision. In this scenario, the new building departments would, at minimum, advocate on behalf of the public interest. The owner, not the architect,

13

would be responsible for coordinating the design work into a coherent whole. He or she could hire a coordinator, but that person would be responsible only to the owner, not to society.

As the ownership of large buildings becomes increasingly sophisticated and owners assemble facilities staffs that exceed the size of their architects', this scenario becomes increasingly plausible. These knowledgeable, well-organized, often quality-oriented owners do not necessarily want (or need) an architect to share the risk of building to achieve a successful result. Unsophisticated owners who are not involved with building construction on a regular basis are in a different situation. They do not have the means to evaluate whether the design services they are receiving meet a benchmark of protection. Some other mechanism would have to be set in place—perhaps a government design or review service—to insure that their buildings met certain minimum standards. The public, on the other hand, would be putting its well-being entirely in the hands of these newly expanded building departments.

The pros and cons of this reconfiguration of the profession are clear. No longer obliged by law to hire government-sanctioned architects, owners would gain unprecedented autonomy, but they would also increase their exposure should something go wrong. The public would both pay for and enjoy the benefits of having a large, mobilized regulatory agency that would intervene in all aspects of the built environment. An adversarial situation would insure that a balance between individual rights and public protection was struck. No longer would that responsibility be vested in an independent person or group of people. The deliberation between public and private interests would become transparent and external to the design process. Designers (formerly called architects) would be responsible for conforming to regulatory requirements, but no longer

14

expected to accept them or believe them to be legitimate expressions of anything other than power. They would be expected to internalize the public's point of view only to the degree that it would help them satisfy their client's needs. The regulators would maintain public standards, but would not actually do the designing.

Restricting the role of architects is certainly plausible. Lots of houses are designed and built without concerned professionals huddling over the plans. This practice is permitted there because the stakes are considered lower than in public or multifamily buildings. Architects would find these adjustments to their professional obligations morally unsatisfying, however. No longer would architectural design be concerned with the widest possible interpretation of goodness—goodness for everyone. In evaluating their own work, designers would consider goodness in much the same way that the legal profession does, as a partisan affair. No longer would anyone straddle the line between what was good for the collective and what was good for the individual. The goodness of a design would be assessed relative to the side for which one worked.

According to this model, design would become less problematic, but only at the expense of engaging fewer considerations. The initial motivation of this strategy—to free architects from the ethical constraints of practice—would be thwarted. Were architects to decide to internalize both the client's needs and those of the public on their own initiative, they would once again become conflicted, but this time the conflict would surround representing oneself dishonestly to one's employers. Thus, although the egoist might be much happier, the morally engaged architect would find this a self-defeating strategy for overcoming his or her professional unease.

The model for reconfiguring the architectural profession presented above would restrict the architect's participation in aspects of the building process and reduce his or her role in society by turning architects into client advocates. In his "Manifesto" of 1991, Christopher Alexander advocated a different model for reforming architectural practice.[18] This model would fundamentally enlarge the scope of work entrusted to the architect. The design professional would resemble a construction czar: contractor, client, artisan, manufacturer, and designer, all rolled into one.

Alexander rejected the model of architectural design as an activity isolated from the actual production of buildings.[19] He argued instead for greatly increasing the architect's responsibilities by merging architecture with construction. The design profession would thereby transcend the dilemmas brought on by its current independence from construction. The architect would assume the role of master builder or master technician— a role with numerous precedents in history, which from time to time is reasserted as a means of shoring up architects' authority. The contracting industry has generally had a good laugh at such egotistical, if not naive, proposals. Wisely, Alexander extends his strategy to include a restructuring of the construction industry as well, upping the ante considerably.

Among Alexander's requirements for restructuring the architectural process are the following:

> No matter how big the building is, the architect does some craft work on every building, with his (or her) own hands.

> The architect controls the flow of money completely: both its distribution at the outset, and the ongoing flow throughout the process.

The architect assumes legal responsibility for the actual construction [of a building].

The architect is leader and artist—but without pride. He or she retains the right to refuse user requests, not based on the architect's ego, but in cases where his (her) grasp of the problem is demonstrably greater. . . .

The architect is committed to make only buildings that are deeply and genuinely liked.

The architect . . . refuses to produce artificial or mechanical repetition. . . .

The architect is committed to daily work and experimentation with techniques of making, forming, fabrication, and construction. . . .

The architect will recognize that the life of construction workers, and their spiritual evolution, is as important as that of the architects. . . .

The architect acknowledges that all building is essentially a religious process.[20]

No doubt the provisions listed above—each of which entails a new moral dilemma—are necessary if the fundamental terms under which buildings are produced are to change substantially. The question for design ethics, however, is whether what would be lost by implementing these changes would outweigh what would be gained.

Although Alexander does not appear to be drawing explicitly from conflict theory, his provisions are out of line with the idea of a balanced contract between the architect and society. Once capitalism's golden rule, "He who has the gold makes the rules," is abandoned and the architect begins to control the money (an unprecedented change in contractual relationships, at least in liberal democracies), it is difficult to imagine how a process of accountability could take hold or could provide a check on this strategy's thoroughgoing paternalism. Review mechanisms within the profession are notoriously (and some would say, inherently) poor at policing such things. The architect would no longer be charged with mediating conflicts between public and private interests because he or she would have a vested interest in a certain outcome. Owners would no longer be allowed to voice their dissatisfaction directly to architects. They would have to contact the building police to arbitrate any disagreements and to protect their rights. Who, then, would insure that both public and private interests were given due consideration?

The presumption has long been that the work of an owner or contractor is not based upon the highly technical knowledge that underpins an architect's work. According to Alexander's thinking, both owners and contractors possesses knowledge that is readily available to the architect. By expanding into what is customarily considered their areas of expertise, architects usurp their responsibility. In doing so, however, architects corrupt their position as guardians of the public interest, not because of this expansion *per se*, but because of the assumption it requires—that architects should retain the right to reject the opinions of others whose grasp of the subject is thought to be inferior to their own. If the right to reject the opinions of others—whether released by the public or simply seized by the architect—is not extended to include public opinion as well, then Alexander's entire project collapses. If the architect caves in to public opinion, he is no better off than when he started; he has merely swapped one master (his own conscience) for another (public consensus). According to this strategy, either architects follow their own conclusions or they suppress what they believe is right and concede to public opinion.

According to the current model of the architecture profession, architects are charged with taking the public will seriously. They must believe in the public's right to influence decisions regarding the built environment—the inevitable outcome of a concept of public service—and, like it or not, must find a way to address public concerns. In Alexander's model, the concept of public service is no longer valid. The public will is considered morally legitimate only if it corresponds with a superior understanding of the relevant issues possessed by the architect. Alexander maintains that the public stands to gain much more than it stands to lose by this arrangement, but what if the public does not share the values of the architect? In Alexander's scheme, society is to blame for the divergence. Architects console themselves with the thought that society simply has not caught up with their superior powers of reasoning.

Perhaps architects stand to benefit from Alexander's model, and perhaps the built environment does as well, but the quality of that environment is only one facet of society's concern. Absent a strong provision for public accountability, how would the wisdom of the architect's judgment ever be tested? The best way for wisdom and good judgment to reveal themselves is through their durability in the face of open scrutiny. The model of the expanded architect reduces significantly the scrutiny built into the conventional construction process.

Part of what is wrong with the notion of expanding or diminishing the role of the architect is that these strategies impose radical changes on the profession. Rather than patiently addressing the profession's most vexing problems, these overhauls trade in one set of known dilemmas for a crop of new ones. While the revolutionary bravado of these proposals is no doubt part of their allure, both do little to sharpen the ethical dimension of architectural practice.

19

The notion that architects are already engaged in a bargain of sorts with society prompts a more conservative approach. Changes to the architect's role would be reflected upon and approved by both parties, or else the bargain would be broken. This concept of a contractual relationship trades on several assumptions: that design professionals are engaged in work that is generally appreciated and understood by society, that these professionals value the trust placed in their work by society, and that architects are willing to modify their activities as society's needs change. Although these conditions may not always be fully realized, they do at least describe a recognizable set of motivations. According to contractarian theory, there is little reason to think that an architect's motivations derive from raw self-interest. Those who believe that professionalism is largely a matter of asserting oneself and coercing the public will are at a loss to explain such apparently counterproductive behavior. The idea of a contract provides a means to distinguish between professional activities that effectively discharge the profession's moral duties and those that lapse into paternalism, insincerity, or coercion. Those who take seriously the idea of a professional engaging in some sort of bargain with the public—a bargain that requires the professional to take the public will seriously, by virtue of the fact that it is the public's will—will find contractarian theory more satisfying.

THE UNEASY ARCHITECT

The critiques of the architecture profession examined to this point have not provided a viable model for reconfiguring the architectural practice in a way that would significantly reduce its ethical dilemmas. The traditional model of the architectural professional could be modified only at the expense of abandoning roles and considerations that architects currently value. An alternative strategy is still needed. The concept of the "uneasy professional," involved in a conflict-ridden, contractual relationship with society, could provide such a strategy.

How might embracing one's uneasiness affect the ethical dilemmas of the architect? To begin with, architects might find comfort in understanding that unease is an inherent part of their role; they can at least cease wondering whether the difficulties of serving both public and private interests, for instance, or the competing values of art and utility are problems that *should* exist in the world or the outgrowth of some condition of practice that needs to be changed. This could have a liberating effect; by accepting these dilemmas as part and parcel of design, architects can begin to address them head-on and with greater confidence.

Embracing the role of mediator in the ethical dilemmas related to building offers another potential benefit. It raises the possibility of locating within the profession a larger social role—a role concerned with something beyond the beauty or quality of the built environment. Architecture could begin to serve as the locus for addressing some of society's most pressing issues, such as the conflict between public and private property rights or the influence of high urban density on human well-being.

Another potential benefit of embracing one's professional unease is an increased realism about the types of dilemmas design alone can solve. The conflicts often faced by architects—concerning, for instance, individual expression versus design guidelines, setback requirements versus maximized leasable area, public access versus the need for security, or Americans with Disabilities Act requirements versus historic character considerations—may be too deeply entrenched in the disparate values of our society to be resolved through good design. This need not reflect poorly on the architect's design skills or talent. It may be seen as a natural outgrowth of a pluralist society—a society in which diversity of values is actually seen as a virtue, something to be allowed and even encouraged. Encouraging diverse points of view on matters of public importance is the only way to protect individual rights while maintaining a sense of community. Inner tension and lack of resolution are built into such societies.

The conflicts that assail the design process are the result of more basic tensions than the architect has means to resolve. The uneasy architect might be concerned about conflicts between individuals and the community and may realistically expect to illuminate these conflicts, but he or she would not expect to transcend them through design.

FACING ISSUES WITHIN THE PROFESSION

Embracing the profession's ethical dilemmas does not mean accepting them without reflection. Many dilemmas would be well-served by moral reflection. One such dilemma involves the notion that architects can effectively act as referees in construction disputes between owners and contractors.[21] Expecting the architect, who is paid by the owner and has invested much of himself in the project's design, to act impartially in the event of a construction dispute is illogical. The owner, who faces a potentially sophisticated adversary in the building contractor, has every right to expect advocacy by the architect during this stage of the building process. The contractor is perfectly capable of voicing his complaints. He needs neither the architect's protection nor benevolence. Demanding that the architect step aside and remain impartial in construction disputes places the less sophisticated owner at a sizable disadvantage. An architect's unease at this situation could be taken as indication that he or she should forego participating in such a dilemmatic situation.

22

Another dilemma for architects that could benefit from moral reflection is the ongoing attempt by interior designers to secure practice legislation for their discipline. Interior designers have sought to elevate themselves into a newly created rank of registered design professional. The architectural profession's collective response to this proposal has been to insist that the ethical issue of public protection is at stake. They argue that interior designers lack the technical training to provide such protections and that to elevate their activities to the rank of licensed professional is both unnecessary and potentially harmful to the public welfare.

According to conflict theory, such "muscling-in" on another's turf is to be expected. Adherents to conflict theory would predict that professions like architecture, which have been able to establish only weak institutional protections, would be more susceptible to such challenges than would professions such as medicine, where relatively strong institutional protections prevail. For conflict theorists, the outcome of such confrontations is determined by the power of the various factions. Indeed, architects' objections to interior designers' registration are often portrayed by the interior design community as a turf-battle and nothing more.

We live in too sophisticated a time to believe that architects' objections to interior designers' licensing have nothing to do with turf, but the question of interest here is whether the conflict is over anything more than turf. What ethical arguments might architects bring to bear on the situation to reinforce their argument against interior designers' receiving professional status?

Interior designers justify seeking the status and protections of state licensure by arguing that what they do engages clients in activities requiring trust, requires specialized knowledge, and places public health and safety at

23

risk. The first of these three conditions of professionalization, regarding the public's trust, simply casts too wide a net to justify state protections in and of itself, but the second and third conditions deserve consideration.

The second condition of professionalization, relating to a specialized knowledge base, raises a quandary for interior designers. The discipline of interior design incorporates two distinctly different groups of practitioners. The first group, commonly referred to as "decorators," traditionally selects and sells furnishings and finishes according to imperatives of taste and, to a lesser extent, performance. To be successfully employed as a decorator, one needs neither formal training nor apprenticeship. To speak of the protections offered to the public by this group of interior designers is to trivialize the concept of public protection.

The second group of practitioners, commonly referred to as "designers," do receive education in both practical and theoretical matters of interior design and engage in theory. They lay tenable claims to a specialized knowledge base characteristic of all professions. The quandary for interior designers is this: if the interior design community favors licensing for both decorators and designers, then interior designers would seem to be acting with blatant disregard for the ethical content of professionalism. If the decorators were granted professional status, then the public will have extended protections to a group that upholds only a trivial concept of professionalism in return. Architects would have no trouble in raising an ethically based objection to such an encroachment on their territory.

Some interior designers who take the conditions of professionalism seriously express a willingness to sacrifice the licensure of decorators and require a certified education, internship, and exam as conditions of registration. Should

24

architects take these educational qualifications seriously? The actual content of interior design education suggests an answer. The accreditation organization for schools of interior design, the Foundation for Interior Design Education and Research (FIDER), lists the following as minimum subject requirements for accreditation,

> Anthropometrics
> Ergonomics
> Proxemics and behavioral theory
> Requirements for special populations
> Interior construction and detailing
> Lighting
> HVAC
> Physical attributes of materials and installation methods
> Building codes
> Fire codes
> Life safety requirements
> Industry product standards
> Business practice
> Specification-writing
> Furnishings[22]

This list of subjects is neither trivial nor—assuming a certain depth of instruction—a mere elevation of common sense. It differs from that contained in architectural curricula in important ways.

In outlining the contents of their professional education, interior designers seem either to be placing great importance on cultivating a singular body of knowledge or to be asking that their unique knowledge base be regarded as a specialized subset of what architects are required to know. This issue is clouded by the fact that the desire for recognition and state protection is so strong within the interior design community that many will argue for whichever is most likely to gain them registration.

If interior designers push only to be recognized as a limited or specialized form of architectural practice, their road to

25

licensure will be easier, because it will intersect the architects' desire for protection of their own status at a lower level of conflict. This route, however, is not without its liabilities. If interior designers maintain that their knowledge base is simply a partial architectural curriculum, they wage an uphill battle to establish its significance to the public. If, on the other hand, interior designers want to insist on the uniqueness of their knowledge base, they will not be able to associate the legitimacy of their skills and knowledge with those of the architect. They will need to establish to the public's satisfaction that interior design registration offers significant public protections in its own right. The interior design community's dithering on this point alludes either to a certain opportunism or to an unfinished project of self-definition.

Regarding the third requirement for professionalization—that interior designers engage serious public-welfare issues—a proponent of interior design licensure argues,

> Suffice it to say that every choice by the interior designers of materials used to embellish or finish the walls, floor, or ceiling of any type of interior, as well as the layout of space and the choice of furniture, furnishings, and equipment to be placed in such a space, has a direct bearing on public-safety issues.[23]

Architects may well question whether arguments like this one are excessive. A more even-handed claim might be that interior designers sometimes make decisions that materially affect public well-being. Conceding this more modest claim falls short of endorsing licensure for interior designers. Architects may ask if the imperative of properly designed interiors in any way matches that of properly designed exterior walls, roofs, load-bearing elements, exits, and the like. It

26

could be argued that interiors are regarded as a distinct discipline precisely because they lack the degree of public importance ascribed to "architectural" elements. On the other hand, certain interior design decisions—say, the space planning and fitting-out of large auditoriums and airports—certainly do stand to materially benefit (or harm) the general public.

The issue turns on the idea of centrality. Architects point to a building's place in the overall environment, its durability and construction, beauty and utility, as the central, ethical concerns of professional practice. Interior designers seem to be pinning their claims to an ethical basis for their practice on the fact that sometimes some designers' work stands to harm the public, if executed without adequate standards of care. To usher in the professionalization of a large body of interior design practitioners on the basis of activities that are marginal to the mainstream of their practice seems unnecessary.

Perhaps interior designers would be on firmer ethical ground if they claim to be a subset, or specialization, of architecture, rather than a distinct discipline. In this scenario, the development of a knowledge base becomes the crucial component in interior designers' claim to professional status. Close examination of current interior design curricula reveals a certain slipperiness in the interior designers' position on the education issue. Completing coursework in Anthropometrics, Ergonomics, and Proxemics may or may not provide a sufficiently distinct technical knowledge base to justify public protection of the title "interior designer." The tempting conclusion to be drawn from this analysis is that interior designers are willing to piggyback their claims for professional licensure onto those of architects' only up to a point; when

27

actually called upon to complete more difficult educational requirements, they change course and maintain instead that their discipline constitutes something different but of equal status to architecture.

Interior designers have been somewhat successful in their attempts to gain equal status with architects and engineers, at least in the eyes of the International Building Code. The Interior Design Alliance, a coalition of interior design organizations, lobbied to have the definition of the term "registered design professional" expanded to include any "individual who is registered or licensed to practice their respective design profession as defined by the statutory requirements of the professional registration laws of the state in which the project is to be constructed."[24] Formerly recognizing only architects and engineers, the phrase "registered design professionals" now applies to interior designers as well.[25] This assertion of equal status is what raises architects' and engineers' ire and may have lead architects to judge the issue of interior design legislation somewhat unfairly. After all, interior designers are not seeking to stamp every construction drawing, only those drawings relating to interior furnishing plans and non-load-bearing construction. Architects who oppose interior designers' parity may want to ask if the question of interior design licensing is not so much about whether interior designers are qualified to stamp such drawings, but whether such drawings need stamping in the first place. Does a formal background in Anthropometrics, Ergonomics, and the like prevent an interior designer from making potentially disastrous design decisions in the same way that a background in structural engineering stands to prevent building collapses or a background in architectural design wards off shoddy or insensitive building practices?

28

There is more to the interior design community's struggle for professional recognition than a war of entrenched interests. The overt struggle against the opposition rallied by architects and engineers has masked an internal problem of self-definition. If interior designers want to defend their claims to licensure on the basis of an ethic of practice, then the industry will have to split into the designers and the decorators, because an ethic is only properly so called when one's actions materially affect public well-being. To speak of an ethic of, say, color selection is nonsense. The decorators' decisions cannot be said meet this requirement, so a split between decorators and designers will be required. But even then, the designers' camp will have to decide between being a specialty of architecture, with all the education that entails, or a completely different discipline, in which case it cannot (without demonstrating its case) legitimately ask to be grouped under the same term with architects as fellow "design professionals"—any more than a chiropractor can claim to be a fellow M.D. or a paralegal, a fellow attorney.

The pairing of specialized knowledge with an ethical imperative determines whether a business activity requires and deserves the public protection of registration. It appears that interior designers can lay a certain legitimate claim to specialized knowledge, but the claim to an ethical imperative is more difficult to establish. Either interior designers must attach the claim of an ethical imperative to the practice of architecture itself, or they must attach it to a rather small and marginal group within the discipline. Both strategies have significant drawbacks: the former course of action deflates the whole enterprise of interior design; the latter risks puffing it up beyond all sense.

This attempt to co-opt public acceptance of one discipline (architecture) for the legitimation of another (interior design) will go largely unexposed as long as architects downplay their important ethical role within society. Many architects, preferring to align themselves more closely with artists than with public servants, do not embrace the role of the ethical architect because they think it will result in undesirable constraints. To the degree that society has only a minimal expectation of the architect as a protector of the public weal, architects may indulge in the pleasures of unbridled artistry. As long as architects shy away from the full potential of the role—by remaining low-key about their values and modest in their claims of working in the public interest—interior designers will be able to successfully press their case.

Architects cannot have it both ways; they cannot continue to expect to enjoy unchallenged public protection for indulging themselves as artists. The interior designers will, in all likelihood, prevail in this event, largely because the interior design professionals are gambling on the chance that no one will scrutinize the ethical content of their claims for professionalization. This is a good bet, as long as architects themselves shun the same scrutiny. By asserting the ethical imperative of protecting the public from undesirable building practices (on aesthetic, structural, *and* moral grounds), architects stand a chance of beating back the interior designers' run at a piece of the business.

The ethical dilemmas faced by architects arise from the conditions under which architecture is practiced. The conflicts between private and public interests that come to the fore in design deliberations typically cannot be resolved without ignoring or arbitrarily narrowing the scope of legitimate claims. The conflict model tempts architects to accept the truth that "power rules" and to quit worrying about making arbitrary decisions, but architects have demonstrated an unwillingness to give in to such temptation, and with good reason. A contractual model, grounded in the notion of professional ethics, generates a more satisfying response to the dilemmas posed by professional practice: why fraudulent practice is unacceptable, why professionals worry over their "duty," why changing the terms of practice is such a hazardous undertaking, and how professionals can justify exclusivity on ethical grounds.

The conclusion that the dilemmas faced in architectural practice are actually good ones to be engaged in sets the stage for looking elsewhere for renewing architecture's moral mission. Having put to the test the idea that architecture's moral decline results from an inappropriate conception of the profession's ethical imperative, the discussion can now turn to theories of the value of architecture itself.

31

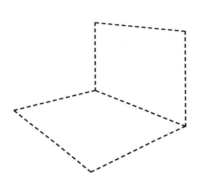

CHAPTER 2 | THEORY

In his *Ten Books on Architecture*, Vitruvius creates a portrait of the architect as a person of broad learning and various talents. Most of the philosophical advice presented by the author, however, is either too antiquated or prosaic to be of much service to contemporary designers. No one can be expected, for example, to examine the livers of a few slaughtered cattle to determine the propitiousness of a proposed site. One Vitruvian assertion, however, has exercised a tenacious hold on the architectural imagination. This is the statement, delivered almost as an afterthought in a discussion of building types, that all architecture "must be built with due reference to durability, convenience, and beauty," in Latin, *firmitas, utilitas,* and *venustas.*[1] All subsequent theories of architecture's basic values have been obliged to grapple with the simple wisdom of Vitruvius' statement.

Despite its longevity, the Vitruvian formulation of what good architecture provides carries with it a built-in quandary. How does one begin to prioritize the imperatives of *firmitas, utilitas,* and *venustas* in cases where these values conflict and a trade-off is required? If these are the basic architectural values, and if they are, indeed, irreducible, then to what superior value does one appeal for judgment when these imperatives pull in opposite directions rather than reinforce each other? An obvious source of judgment is one's ethics.

As many of his readers have observed, Vitruvius possessed an unreflective temperament. He ignored the possibility that conflicts between the irreducible values of *firmitas, utilitas*, and *venustas* would be a source of dismay for architects seeking guidance in the creation of good buildings. Vitruvius was satisfied that a properly prepared architect would possess the necessary skills to resolve such conflicts. In addition to a liberal, practical knowledge base, the adequate education of an architect would include an inculcation of virtues. An architect would be "high-minded and not self-assuming . . . courteous, just, and honest without avariciousness" and would "keep up his position by cherishing a good reputation."[2] Vitruvius did not think that such preparation would be an easy matter, but neither did he perceive the logical problem entailed in holding proper preparation to be the solution to the problem of conflicting values.

The logical problem that arises from Vitruvius' formulation is this: if good buildings result from the deliberations of knowledgeable and virtuous architects, then it follows that a person could be a good architect without having actually designed any buildings, simply by virtue of the fact that he or she is adequately educated and of good moral fiber. This conclusion, however, is at odds with commonsense views of how an architect's reputation is made. Ordinarily, we would think that one's status as a good architect depended on the merits of one's buildings. We may go with Vitruvius on this issue and still hold a weaker position, that a good building is an *indicator* of the presence of a good architect, we just cannot hold that one's capabilities as an architect are defined by one's buildings without circularity.

We might reasonably ask, what else—in addition to one's built work—should be required to establish one's worth as an architect. Must the good architect also be able to demonstrate that he or she is a benevolent employer, prudent with finances, or a talented draftsperson? Probably not. These traits may be desirable, or make architects more likely to produce good designs, but the reputations of many otherwise highly regarded architects would suffer considerably if these traits were held out to be requirements of a good architect. Rather, many practitioners prove themselves to be good architects despite a glaring lack of some of these corollary traits.

This is not the only problem generated by Vitruvius' response to the issue of irreducible and conflicting architectural values. How can someone who is considered a good architect still produce a bad building from time to time? When the definition of good architecture is not made a function of the architect's preparation and character, this problem does not arise.

Vitruvius may well have gotten the dependency relationship between good architecture and the good architect backwards in his *Ten Books*. Practitioners are regarded as good architects because they have designed buildings that are widely recognized as good. With the relationship stated this way, the problem of how a good architect could design the occasional bad building disappears. Enough bad buildings and one's reputation sags. Furthermore, one might be regarded as a poor architect but luck into an occasional good design without raising an ontological problem. The problem of circularity disappears. Along with it, however, goes the solution to the problem of conflicting values—that skill is all that is needed to guide architects through conflicts in values. Design skill is certainly necessary, but not sufficient in and of itself. Clearly, the problem of weighing the values of *firmitas, utilitas,* and *venustas* is more complex than Vitruvius would have it appear.

Subsequent architects and theorists have contended with the problem of conflicting architectural values in several ways. Some have insisted that, although Vitruvius was correct about the plurality of values, one value can always be identified as superior to the others; its trump value does the necessary prioritizing. Others have argued against the Vitruvian idea of the irreducibility of architectural values, proposing instead a unity of values, such as function and beauty. A third, and more recent, response to the problem of multiple and conflicting values in architecture asserts that one should withdraw from the inevitable compromise between values—the residue of a bankrupt humanist ideology—and instead concentrate design efforts on breaking up this ancient antagonism. Each of these ideas has something to offer the Vitruvian dilemma.

PLURAL VALUES

Robert Venturi set the stage in recent times for asserting the plurality of basic architectural values with his assertion that "architecture is necessarily complex and contradictory in its very inclusion of the traditional Vitruvian elements of commodity, firmness, and delight."[3] Following his lead, an embrace of mixed and possibly conflicting values came to characterize the developing postmodern sensibility to such an extent that architectural theorist Charles Jencks could assert, "pluralism is the Post-Modern ideology above all others."[4]

There was really nothing new, however, about this affirmation of the Vitruvian diversity of architecture's values. Leon Battista Alberti echoes Vitruvius on this point almost word for word, although he went on to address the problem of a conflict of values, claiming that when utility and structure were adequately addressed, beauty was an almost inevitable result.[5] Andrea Palladio, too, subscribed to the Vitruvian values. He dispatched the problem of potential conflicts by arguing that reason would perform the function of supreme arbiter between the demands of *venustas* and *utilitas*. In his 1624

Elements of Architecture, Henry Wotton took up the same position. "The end is to build well," he wrote. "Well building hath three conditions: *Commoditie, Firmenes*, and *Delight* . . . the place of every part, is to be determined by use."[6] Following Wotton, Sir William Chambers expressed much the same idea, arguing that beauty should be justified in terms of the utilitarian benefits it bestows on man's well-being.[7] While acknowledging the potential for conflict among architectural values, Karl Friedrich Schinkel gave priority to *venustas*, maintaining, "the task of architecture is to make something practical, useful, and functional into something beautiful."[8]

The turn away from the Vitruvian tradition by nineteenth-century rationalists, which subsequently evolved into modernist functionalism, has made the postmodern adoption of a plurality of values seem more like an avant-garde rejectionist movement than a simple return to earlier, conservative values. To be sure, postmodernists gave the problem a new spin by insisting not only on the independence of *firmitas, utilitas*, and *venustas*, but on the value of their being independent as well. The plurality of Vitruvian values was not only a fact resulting from the inability to reduce *firmitas, utilitas*, and *venustas* to a single value, but it was considered a morally good thing in and of itself.

The term "pluralism" has a democratic ring, something easily endorsed in an age suspicious of united fronts. Does postmodernism, however, endorse the "cooperation among equals" that we associate with political pluralism, or does it support—as many have charged—only a pluralism among the aesthetic elite? The famed double-coding of postmodernist monuments, whereby a building talks down to or up to its audience depending on their level of sophistication, is certainly lost on most. But even so, this shortcoming may not warrant a wholesale condemnation of the postmodern movement.

More problematic for postmodern pluralism—especially as it applies to *venustas*, or aesthetic judgment—is that the movement falls apart once a basis of agreement between people becomes too particularized or fragmented. In the United States, where Democrats, Republicans, Reform Party members, and other groups continue to slug it out, pluralism functions as a valuable tool for insuring the well-being of society. Some general points of agreement—what constitutes basic human rights, what the social value of cooperation is, what a just society looks like—that are shared by all groups prevent a descent into anarchy. Fear of the consequences of not agreeing helps to sustain the whole enterprise. Without some points of widespread agreement save a commitment to pluralism itself, no compelling reason could be found to prevent individuals from pursuing their own political agendas. In the case of artistic pluralism, however, no such urgency informs a need to agree. Artistic differences do not result in civil wars. Some viewpoints may be considered more informed than others, but all are without the force of an ethical imperative behind them. This is the paradox of postmodern pluralism. Due to what it regards as the moralistic excesses of modernism, postmodernism keeps morality out of the discussion of artistic decisions. By claiming allegiance to the ethic of pluralism, it attempts to claim a moral basis for otherwise arbitrary preferences and hence greater social relevance. Pluralism in architecture, however, is not the same as pluralism in politics. Pluralism in art cannot count on any further relevance within the realm of ethics.[9]

With modernism, art and utility were deliberately intertwined; with postmodernism, they are liberated from one another and from concerns of durability. The movement that received much of its impetus from the false portrayal of modernism's social benefits has been loathe to fall into the trap of moralizing its art. Some say it makes no such claims, that its only claims are for the liberation of art; social benefit is at best a by-product of such action. These architects were happy to stick to art and technique, leaving morality to the politicians.

Without some claim to morality, however, even the phrase "building well" loses its normative meaning. One practitioner might say it means responding to what people like. Another might argue it means challenging people visually. Still another might maintain that it means following the modernist agenda. To say that everyone is equally correct smacks of intellectual dishonesty or cowardice. Yet why would an architect feel motivated to find a common area of agreement? Postmodernism cannot restrict the terms of the debate without disavowing its most fundamental proposition of pluralism. To liberate art from morality and then to endorse pluralism in art without simultaneously referring to reasons for commonality is to deny the role of widespread agreement in critical evaluation. Anyone's opinion is as valid as anyone else's, and no compelling moral reason for solidarity can be summoned without disavowing the one value to which the postmodernist was willing to commit. One could try, instead, to summon artistic reasons for solidarity, but these reasons will have to compete with everyone's personal reasons and agendas.

Another result of endorsing pluralism is that one form of monism—the modernist emphasis on function—is replaced by another—the postmodernist emphasis on diversity. The propensity of a design solution to promote diversity becomes the ultimate criterion of its goodness—an odd measure of design excellence. Before postmodernism burst on the scene, we would have been more likely to judge a design excellent by how well it combined beauty, functionality, and structural integrity, rather than by how many different interpretations we could wring out of it. Although pluralism may form the bedrock

41

of liberal democracies, it is not their only value. Those who welcomed postmodernism's rehabilitation of values other than function may be dismayed by postmodernism's inability to articulate a wide set of values other than pluralism itself. Embracing pluralism as a way to ground a renewed assertion of a diversity of values is not a bad strategy, but it could do with some reinforcements.

David Watkin sought to bolster the postmodernist separation of art and utility by showing supposedly moral sentiments on the part of modernism's precursors and proponents to be, in actuality, thinly disguised aesthetic preference.[10] But this, too, falls short of providing a rationale for proceeding in the face of conflicting values. Watkin leaves the impression that moral arguments are inherently out of place in justifying aesthetic preference, but this impression is somewhat undermined by the trouble even proponents of pluralism of value have in keeping morality out of the discussion. While Venturi's opening sentence in *Complexity and Contradiction*, "I like complexity and contradiction in architecture," establishes the basis for a successful aesthetic challenge to the modernist attempt to unify style and morality, morality enters through the back door, through the ambitious meanings he assigns to the terms "complexity" and "contradiction."[11] From the onset, he refers to complexity and contradiction as artistic problems arising out of an attitude of inclusion: "Contradictions can represent the exceptional inconsistency that modifies the otherwise consistent order, or they can represent inconsistencies throughout the order as a whole."[12]

Not content to let them stand as merely internal, artistic values, Venturi eventually makes complexity and contradiction out to be something much more inclusive. He advocates "genuinely complex programs."[13] If morality touches on anything in architecture, it touches on a building's program-matic function and utility. Venturi cannot rely on the good in artistic complexity to carry over into an argument for programmatic complexity if he is maintaining the independence of artistic merit from moral judgment. Programmatic complexity must find justification elsewhere, and this is something he does not provide. The word "genuinely" is the key to morality's appearance in his argument. The evaluative term is meant to distinguish between pretense and reality, but with Venturi it contains a normative sense of discriminating between a self-serving cover-up and humbly allowing the full bite of the situation to be felt and expressed, even if it be unpleasant. His argument in favor of programmatic complexity either needs to discard "genuinely" if it is to leave morality out of the discussion of art, or it needs to develop some durable criteria for distinguishing false simplicity from real complexity. Venturi wants his argument to hold more force than to be merely about artistic decisions, but he wants his artistic argument to do the work. If art is liberated from function, then function is liberated from art, and so is its justification. On the other hand, if a connection exists between art and morality, it must run both ways.

The postmodern argument has by no means sufficiently buoyed the concept of multiple architectural values to escape the modernist problem of aesthetic value being subsumed by utility. Indeed, Venturi backs off from even trying, by eventually allowing that in case of a conflict, preference should be given to utility.[14] For Venturi, this was an expression of humility and pragmatism, but it also runs the risk of ultimately allying him with the functionalist camp. The basic humanity of his sentiment begins to break down as utility begins to dominate, resulting in a severe, utilitarian functionalism in

43

which beauty and structure are given short shrift. Limitations must be devised to prevent a rampant, narrow functionalism from ruining the built environment, yet if one places curbs on the degree to which utility can dominate, and if those curbs are based on structural and aesthetic criteria, then the dilemma remains intact and nothing has been achieved by giving preference to utility in cases of conflict.

Architectural postmodernism must return once again to its commitment to pluralism and demonstrate its own achievements for ethical justification. This may be enough to keep the movement in play, but it is not enough to allow it a central place as architecture changes and develops with the times. The history of how quickly its artistic and moral imperatives flowered and burned out (roughly ten years) may be evidence enough. Postmodernism has been crowded out by deconstruction, neo-traditionalism, and neo-modernism. The first shares, in an odd way, postmodernism's pluralism. The second and third reassert the unity of the beautiful and the functional.

THE UNITY OF VALUES

Asserting the unity of the beautiful and the useful can derive from any of several premises. Alberti argued, "beauty is some inherent property [of the] reasoned harmony of all the parts within a body."[15] This "reasoned harmony" represents a synthesis of the Vitruvian values and, hence, unites them. Others of a less poetic temperament would simply enforce the unity of values by culling out those examples that create conflict. This was Wotton's and Chamber's solution. The innovation modernism brought to the problem of conflicting values was the commitment to deriving beauty directly from function. The development of functionalist theory from J.-N.-L. Durand to its flowering under Le Corbusier, Walter

Gropius, Sigfried Giedion, Bruno Taut, and Nicholas Pevsner has been well-documented by others.[16] Modernism's insistence on unifying architecture's goods imparted a certain earnestness—a sense of conviction—noticeably missing from the postmodern outlook. Distrust of this earnestness is a hallmark of postmodernism.[17]

Some architectural theorists would like to recapture the sense of a strong moral mission in architecture. Karsten Harries, for example, wrote in *The Ethical Function of Architecture*, of his distress over the diminished state of architecture's moral ambitions.[18] Nostalgic for the conviction and certainty that Wright, Mies, Le Corbusier, Gropius, and other pioneers of the modern movement expressed for their work—that their work would improve the built environment and benefit mankind—Harries would like to recapture the modernist certainty that the aim of architecture is, at least in part, to improve the world. He would agree with Watkin and Venturi that the decline in emphasis on morality in architectural theory is due to the ascendance of the concept of the aesthetic independence of architecture, but Harries would disagree about the desirability of this development.

Harries dissected the current condition of architecture as follows:

> Unfortunately, the hopes of the functionalist not withstanding, not only is there no assurance that an economic and efficient solution to practical problems will also be aesthetically pleasing, but given the aesthetics of purity, there is no chance that modern architecture's marriage of art and engineering will be free of tension and compromise ... on the aesthetic approach the beauty of a building has to appear as something added on to what necessity dictates as decoration in a broad sense. The tensions that result from this mingling of pragmatic and aesthetic concerns all but rule out aesthetic completeness.[19]

45

For Harries' observation to be damning, one must first subscribe to the idea that "aesthetic completeness" is one of the goods. This is debatable. One need only recall Venturi's preference for complexity and contradiction to realize that aesthetic incompleteness may be considered of greater value than are unity and repose. But assuming that excessive internal tension may well be undesirable, Harries must posit an alternative vision of architecture's value free of potentially conflicting terms if he is to present a better model. Finding functionalism sufficiently discredited, the author tries a different approach to resuscitating modernism's sense of conviction.

Harries takes up a Heideggerian metaphysical approach, which seeks to redefine architecture by reintroducing the most elemental concepts with which it is associated: "dwelling," "place," "the terror of time," and "presentness."[20] By reasserting the metaphysics of architecture, Harries undercuts the entire issue of conflicting values. In the deepest possible meaning of these terms may well reside an antidote to the facile character of modernity, but such an approach is not without its pitfalls. Most notably, it resists verification and objective evaluation. Who is to say when one has grasped the deepest meaning of "dwelling"? For those who require external verification, this highly subjective and ultimately self-referential strategy will fall short.[21]

Looking elsewhere, we can find in Platonic thought a sense of conviction that is missing in the postmodern outlook. Rather than attempting to derive beauty from utility, as the modernists did, Plato would simply have asserted that the beautiful must be good.[22] This idea is not merely of antiquarian interest. In his *Tractatus*, Wittgenstein asserted this idea rather cryptically, saying, "Ethics and aesthetics are one and the same."[23] This idea was given a thorough renovation in the twentieth century by G. E. Moore, who thought that the question of whether something is truly beautiful or not "depends upon the *objective* question whether the whole in question is or is not truly good. . . . It appears probable that the beautiful should be *defined* as that of which the admiring contemplation is good in itself."[24] Some scholars take the beautiful as evidence of the good. Others see the beautiful and the good as two sides of the same coin. Vacillation between these conceptions may well be endemic to such unity theories.

E. H. Gombrich notes an analogy between expressions of moral value and those of artistic value that involve certain virtues. In the essay "Visual Metaphors of Value in Art," he notes that the two kinds of expression can become intertwined. As an example, he cites Alberti's discussion of "noble simplicity," the concept that what is forsaken can be as important as what is engaged. According to Gombrich, "Art now stands in a cultural context in which an expectation aroused and denied can itself be expressive of values."[25] Elsewhere, Gombrich notes modernism's employment of the metaphor of "clean lines" to denote value. Vulgar, childish indulgences are resisted for the sake of greater self-control both in art and in morality. Distaste for "false sentiment" in art, as in life, possesses moral overtones.

Gombrich's argument takes a strange turn, however. He claims that the judgment of "false sentiment" is not due to any fault in the work of art, but rather to our being victims of the tendency of civilization to narrow the range of emotions acceptable to display. Gombrich holds cultural repression responsible for certain perceptions, thus belittling the object of these thoughts. Gombrich's insights into the similarities between moral and aesthetic values are promising, but one wonders as a result of his strange turn, if a foray into utter subjectivity is their inevitable result.

47

For those wishing to revive the sense of ethical conviction felt by early modernists, still another possibility is to follow Viollet-le-duc into a tectonic interpretation of architecture's goods.[26] Viollet-le-duc arrived at his value system through a deep-seated appreciation for the structural beauty of French Gothic architecture. Beauty was not simply subordinate to structure. It was the outgrowth of the proper expression of structure itself. According to this outlook, only two independent architectural values exist: structure and function. Given that we often hold a special place for the beauty that arises out of sophisticated structure—think of Viollet-le-duc's prized Gothic cathedrals or the Golden Gate Bridge—and forgetting for a moment the limitations on aesthetic pleasure that such an approach would require, the potential conflict between structure/beauty and function must be addressed. Viollet-le-duc narrows the conflict by claiming that only one truly right structure exists for any given situation, thus invoking an argument of structural determinism. Given that structure, in his system, now incorporates both beauty and an idealist outlook regarding structural choice, to insist on the equal importance of function would be both intolerable and immoral.

Other theorists have claimed that the conflict between function and beauty as expressed through structure is a result of falling short of the model of structural rationality. From this perspective, Viollet-le-duc can be seen as having built upon the theories of Abbé Laugier. Laugier held that the perception of beauty naturally arises as the building assumes its most elemental form as basic, primitive enclosure.[27] The simple post and beam, the pitched roof, the porch; these were the forms that the human psyche responds to and perceives as beautiful. As a building moves away from these elemental forms— through the addition of such dreaded motifs as the engaged column, for instance—beauty recedes. Viollet-le-duc chose a more sophisticated model in the Gothic cathedral, but the basic argument is the same.

The determinist aspect of Viollet-le-duc's argument seems silly today, as does his assertion; no one seriously thinks that an ideal structure exists for every building project or that every structure has an inherent beauty that need only to be given expression. Yet the idea that beauty can be considered an outgrowth of either function or structure is still viable. When *firmitas* and *venustas* achieve confluence, architecture achieves some of its more rapturous moments. Furthermore, Viollet-le-duc's insistence that architecture is fundamentally driven by a concern with certain material objects and not merely with what these objects provide as instruments of function makes an important point against functionalism. Although his excessive rhetoric is best discarded, his passion for buildings is not.

A final means of conceiving of the unity of values needed to recapture modernism's sense of moral conviction can be found in the assertion of aesthetic superiority.[28] According to this way of thinking, the aesthetic does not simply operate independent of function, as in the pluralist approach; nor is the beautiful merely evidence of the good, as it was for Plato. Rather, perception of beauty precedes recognition of moral worth.

Art critic Paul Tillich argued that the aesthetic function is identical to cognition. In other words, to see, hear, and taste, and to understand that one is seeing, hearing, and tasting, is to have an aesthetic experience of seeing, hearing, and tasting. Tillich writes,

> Both (cognitive and aesthetic functions) receive reality without changing it as such. They transform it into images, concepts, words, odors. But they do not transform the objects as such. . . . The theoretical transforma-

tion of what is given to us does not transform the actual state of the given. It transforms the content of the ordinary encounter into an object of cognitive or aesthetic reception.[29]

It is at least worth doubting the truth of his statement that the awareness of an experience is the same thing as having an aesthetic experience. Tillich needs this to be true, however, if he is to press his case for the inextricable closeness of aesthetic experience and cognition.

Art theorist Clive Bell, by contrast, grounds aesthetic experience in high hedonism.[30] By making the experience of beauty nothing but pleasure, Bell places art and aesthetic experience out of the reach of moral judgment. His argument follows in the tradition of John Stuart Mill's distinction between higher and lower pleasures and assumes the same liabilities. Who is qualified to draw the line between higher and lower pleasures?

Philosopher José Ortega y Gasset thought art serves a "function," but not in any ordinary meaning of the word:

> Now then, imagine the importance of a language or system of expressive signs whose function was not to tell us about things but to present them to us in the act of executing themselves. Art is just such a language; this is what art does. The aesthetic object is inwardness as such—it is each thing as "I" . . . a work of art affords the peculiar pleasure we call esthetic by making it seem that the inwardness of things, their executant reality, is opened to us.[31]

Like Ortega, R. G. Collingwood, Gombrich, and Herbert Read maintain that art is a form of communication.[32] All of these communication theories, however, share the difficulty of explaining what, in fact, is being communicated, and furthermore, why we tend to value art and aesthetic experience for its own sake. Regular forms of communication tend to be valued instrumentally, for how well they facilitate people's getting along with each other and getting the things they want.

More recently, philosopher of art Marcia Eaton suggests several scenarios for how aesthetics could be considered superior or "prior" to ethics.[33] Aesthetics could precede ethics if it held a formal priority—that is, if to understand things ethically required organizing them into a format or schema that was understood aesthetically—or if it held a psychological or behavioral priority, in which the failure to be able to regard things aesthetically resulted in the inability to look at things from a moral point of view. She rejected both of these possibilities, embracing instead the concept of "conceptual interdependence."[34] She maintains, "In order to understand morality and thus become a mature moral person, one's action must have both appropriate style and content, and this requires aesthetic skills."[35] She observes,

> Both aesthetic and moral sensitivity are demanded in making judgments such as "This situation calls for bold action" or "This situation calls for subtlety." Great music as well as great literature helps one to learn to make such distinctions.[36]

By using words such as "boldness" and "subtlety," Eaton identifies a class of concepts embodying both ethical and aesthetic judgments. This idea of conceptual interdependence holds promise, but it falls far short of justifying artistic priority. It is more likely to lead to another form of pluralism.

The neo-traditionalist movement provides a unity theory of its own, by asserting the universal appeal of the architecture that originated in ancient Greece. For neo-traditionalists such as Leon Krier, the use of these motifs which have withstood the test of time results in an architecture at once beautiful and

51

responsive to people's needs. The goal of traditional design is "mainly to conceive, realize and maintain a solid, lasting, comfortable, and possibly beautiful common world." Fundamental aesthetic and ethical principles are considered to be "of universal value . . . transcending time and space, climates and civilization."[37] This ideal provides the architect with a moral imperative.

Timelessness is certainly a value architects can rally around, but what is really meant by this word and what are the implications of adhering to it as a primary source of value? The notion that anything is truly timeless has taken such a hit since Hegel initiated the large-scale project of historicizing everything that one is hesitant to speak of anything but the physical properties of matter as timeless. Antiessentialism is the ruling paradigm of the day. So it seems unlikely that Krier is holding onto an ahistorical notion of architecture as timeless. He speaks of the classical idiom as something durable, and he is on reasonably firm ground here. Krier must demonstrate, however, the unique correspondence between the human perception of corporeal beauty and classicism. Although this correspondence may not be so hard to demonstrate—indeed, it has been demonstrated repeatedly with regard to the four orders of classical architecture—the notion that the classical system is the only system to correspond to ideals of beauty does not follow. As soon as we grant that humans may derive notions of beauty from examples other than the human body— from spider webs, the Grand Canyon, antelopes, and architecture itself—then the argument no longer leads inexorably to classicism.

Neo-traditionalists bolster their preferences for classicism with two additional arguments. The first is that classicism provides a ready set of motifs and conventions that people respond to and understand. This assertions relies heavily on convention. While not necessarily a bad thing, the potential brittleness of neo-traditional theory manifests itself when architects are called upon to design for foreign locales or for building types or contexts not anticipated by the ancients or their Renaissance admirers. The Victorians faced the same dilemma when it came to railroad stations and bridges that neo-traditionalist architects face today in the design of airports and skyscrapers. Although flexible, the classical vocabulary is not *that* flexible. In these situations, neo-traditionalists can no longer rely on established conventions; they are obliged to move into new and uncharted territory along with everyone else.

The second argument that neo-traditionalists employ to justify their preferences is that classicism constitutes a more robust system than any other. They assert, with good reason, that in the debate between classicism and modernism, classicism is by far the more supple and forgiving style. They maintain that even a mediocre effort in the classical idiom will turn out decently, while a mediocre effort in the modern style will turn out poorly. This second, more modest, claim is more sustainable, but fails to capture the sense of moral conviction that arguments based on timelessness enjoy.

This survey of theories summoned in the past to bolster the cause of the unity of architectural values has not identified prospects likely to be resilient in the face of the demands of utility. Those, like Harries, who would recapture the sense of conviction characteristic of modernism's heyday are likely to lead once again toward a discredited functionalism. The one thing that the theories of Heideggerian metaphysics, identity, communication, Platonic idealism, and aesthetic priority do have going for them is that they all express, in various ways, the importance of aesthetic experience that theories of utility cannot. Theories of utility must describe the value of art and aesthetic experience in terms of what they contribute to some other human good—be it happiness, a certain standard of living, the greatest good for the greatest number, or some other function—thus driving a wedge between the work of art and its value. Despite its excesses and difficulties, one should not discard the idea of aesthetic superiority too quickly. The idea has the ability to summon the passion and intimacy many would like to secure for their art and to bolster a sense of conviction often found to be lacking in pluralist conceptions of architectural values.

WITHDRAWAL

The third branch of theory asserts that both modernists and postmodernists are engaged in a game of endless compromise between form and function and that art cannot find its place within these confines. Proponents of this theory want to withdraw from this game altogether. Jorge Silvetti expresses this sentiment when he writes,

> Perhaps through the exercise of this criticism it will be possible to produce the "subtle subversion" that Barthes suggests as a possible solution to the contradictions of art; that is to say, the subversion that does not accept the play with opposites that are merely accomplices within the same structure (i.e. the endless oscillation between formalism and functionalism), but one that seeks another term beyond the game of oppositions, a term not of synthesis but of an eccentricity that frustrates false oppositions.[38]

In Silvetti's view, the "oscillations" in architecture that have taken place since the Enlightenment—neoclassicism, the Gothic Revival, modernism, postmodernism, and the like—are lumped under the rubric of humanism.[39] What is so bad about humanism, according to these outlooks, is that it tends to reinforce the status quo, providing no means for escape from this "play with opposites."[40]

In his 1924 *The Architecture of Humanism*, Geoffrey Scott maintained that the importance of humanism lies in the outlook it encourages, which places man at center stage. "Humanism," he writes, "is the effort of men to think, to feel, and to act for themselves, and to abide by the logic of [the] results."[41] Humanism tends to discourage moral conceptions based on supernatural or metaphysical grounds; it makes man the originator and the measure of all things. Man "may construct, within the world as it is, a pattern of the world as he would have it."[42] Scott maintains that the humanist value system precedes and underlies any conception of architecture, the arts, philosophy, and life. This system is consistent with the Vitruvian conception of architectural values: "Architecture is a focus where three separate purposes have converged (commodity, firmness, and delight)." Only by endorsing the humanist point of view, Scott maintains, could these three potentially conflicting terms be allowed to persist. They persist because they sum up more important human ends than any other unified theory presented. These ends are deemed so important that the prospect of conflict is more agreeable than that of letting any one of them fall to the wayside. Modern functionalists have forgotten this fact. According to Scott, "Theory and criticism have largely failed because they try to force an unreal unity of aim."[43]

Scott's version of humanism would act as a brake against those who forget that architects build for actual man, as opposed to an ideal. This is humanism's great strength, and this is also where it receives its drubbing. Actual humans bring with them all sorts of undesirable baggage; they value creature comforts and security and often settle for less than the ideal. Their means generally involve compromise and incrementalism. They tend to shirk from big challenges. They are frivolous, big-hearted, sentimental, easily manipulated, and like things with beginnings and ends. Because it affirms actual human beings, humanism is limited in the critiques it can make of the status quo. This is why it is regarded as apologist. Humanism's affirmation of humans "as is" means a shuttling back to this origin, no matter how far afield one's thinking may wish to lead—hence, the endless oscillation of which Silvetti speaks. Modernism swings towards function; postmodernism swings towards form.

Having diagnosed the humanist form-function balance to be an exhausted project, Peter Eisenman attempts to discard it in favor of something he can pursue without compromise. He would prefer to engage in a posthumanist architecture where human needs are dislocated from their traditional centrality and the project of creating the object itself—not the object's effects on mankind—becomes architecture's focus.[44] The question arises, however, as to whether an architect can leave behind all the claims of form and function and still make something that can be called architecture? The very decision to de-center the human being falls within the humanist tradition of engaging in a critical dialogue with humanist ideals. To change the humanist balance, one must at least think this is a potentially good thing to do. But good according to what standard? Good for mankind? Good for the objects created? Good for those involved in the critical project?

Eventually, posthumanism needs to be accountable to something. Posthumanists certainly are not making appeals to God or to the greatest good for the greatest number. They disdain such appeals as symptoms of the tradition from which they wish to withdraw. If displacing man from the center means that, say, all living things are now considered central, then this is simply an enlargement of the established project of environmental ethics. If this is not the measure, then what is? Eisenman, like the poststructuralist philosopher Jacques Derrida and the members of the Frankfurt School, would presumably like the measure of success to be internal, so that a project is evaluated according to its own theory of success. Eisenman writes, "This new theoretical base changes the humanist balance of form/function to a dialectical relationship within the evolution of form itself."[45] Such standards of success, however, do not admit of verification. Echoing this concern, Mary McLeod worries,

> In a world of endless textuality, how can the institutional and material causes of representation—and oppression— ever be determined or examined sufficiently to be countered? In a world without truth, history, or consensus, what is the basis or criterion for action? In other words, how does one choose the objects, strategies, and goals of subversion? Is there any way to avoid total relativism—a sense that anything goes?[46]

What do poststructuralists like Silvetti and Eisenman propose in place of humanism? Rather than aim for timeless beauty, they seek interesting collisions. They seek to fragment things to such a degree that people are challenged and defeated in their ongoing attempts to mentally possess the world around them. Bernard Tschumi affirms,

> The (new) architecture of pleasure lies where conceptual and spatial paradoxes merge in the middle of delight, where architectural language breaks into a thousand pieces, where the elements of architecture are dismantled and its rules transgressed. No metaphorical paradise here, but discomfort and unbalanced expectations. . . . Such architecture is perverse because its real significance lies outside any utility or purpose and ultimately is not even necessarily aimed at giving pleasure."[47]

57

No longer a means to elicit a fresh perspective on the world, dishabituation becomes an end in itself.

The value-laden activity of judging a building according to function or beauty is exchanged for the opportunity to engage in the value-free activity of reading architecture as a text. This activity of "reading" encourages a high-degree of intellectual detachment from the object at hand. There is never the slightest interest in discerning whether all these dishabituating, dislocating moves are actually achieving something important for mankind. Indeed, the critical positions assumed by posthumanism's proponents are notably apolitical and asocial. As McLeod notes, these positions "have erred . . . in their abjuration of all realms of the social and in their assumption that form remains either a critical or affirmative tool independent of social and economic processes."[48] The clearest justification for such moves is that they allow the people making them to engage in the kinds of critical enterprises they find interesting. The champions of posthumanist withdrawal would do well to heed Richard Rorty's observation that similar kinds of enterprises by leftist intellectuals serve no social purpose:

> More generally, one should see the intellectual *qua* intellectual as having a special, idiosyncratic need—a need for the ineffable, the sublime, a need to go beyond the limits, a need to use words which are not part of anybody's language-game, any social institution. But one should not see the intellectual as serving a *social* purpose when he fulfills this need. Social purposes are served, just as Habermas says, by finding beautiful ways of harmonizing interests, rather than sublime ways of detaching oneself from others' interests. The attempt of leftist intellectuals to pretend that the avant-garde is serving the wretched of the earth by fighting free of the eerily beautiful is a hopeless attempt to make the special needs of the intellectual and the social needs of his community coincide.[49]

To criticize posthumanists for their inability to make a social contribution falls short of advocating a return to the same old humanism of Geoffrey Scott. Scott's humanism, too, is a much better critique than a construction. Scott faces the problem of how to justify the place of *venustas* in a world largely measured by utility. His justification both for preserving the independence of the aesthetic dimension and for the superiority of humanist architecture culminates in his claim that, "We have transcribed ourselves into terms of architecture."[50] This is a magnificent premise for the creation and evaluation of architecture according to a set of values—a set of values we might very much like to subscribe to and champion—but this concept is too vague to provide any real framework for design. Short of the Caryatid Porch on the Erechtheion, actual representations of human form in architecture are rare. Scott may have had in mind some level of abstraction, perhaps in the sense of the classical orders' embodiment of the proportions of the human body. This would circumscribe the aesthetic dimension of architecture, returning it to the renaissance/neoclassical models of which Scott is so fond. It serves as a reason for preferring classicism, but also for excluding such great buildings as Dulles Airport for appreciation. The concept of "transcrib[ing] ourselves in terms of architecture" is vacuous.

By failing to acknowledge the enormous role that convention plays in the communication and perception of aesthetic effect, Scott fails where posthumanist critics score their biggest points. Posthumanists have accurately charged that humanism is limited in its ability to stand back and regard itself critically, and they have presented serious works of architecture that act as a corrective. Eisenman's Wexner Center, Tschumi's Parc de la Villette pavilions, and Zaha Hadid's angular compositions demonstrate that challenging the role of convention in communication and perception holds potential for opening up architecture to fresh, exciting observations. What posthumanist architects are not able to demonstrate is whether this opening up serves any end beyond itself.

RETURNING TO VITRUVIUS

Certainly, the modernist ideal of an ethically unified architecture has yet to be rehabilitated from its disrepute. Watkin was amply justified in excoriating its tendency "to deny or falsify the role of aesthetic motivation and to claim instead guidance from considerations of 'naturalness,' utility, functional advantage, and social, moral, and political necessity, or simply from correspondence with the 'spirit of the age.'"[51] Modernism's attempted synthesis of art and utility all too often took more than it gave; it required people to give up traditions, familiarities, and forms that contributed much meaning in life and offered in return both the prospect of a life suffused with art and a rationally, ergonomically, and economically devised environment. Rather than bringing art into everyday life, areas of life that had formerly been reserved for art became dominated by utility—or, just as bad, utility was tortured by attempts to mold it into art.[52] Modernism lost its moral imperative when it became obvious to enough people that it was not keeping up its end of the bargain.

Several attempts to redefine the relationship of architectural values for architecture following the collapse modernism's moral imperative have been discussed here. Pluralism is not able to count on the urgent need for agreement that political pluralism trades on, and it compartmentalizes the aesthetic realm. Those wishing to reinstate a large role for art and aesthetics against the claims of utility lack strong arguments. Their one strength is that the intimacy between ethics and aesthetics has a certain resonance that other theories fail to capture. Humanism appears to rely on a justification that, ironically, does not square with actual human experience. Posthumanist theories tend to descend into radical subjectivity; when seeking justification in some kind of cultural good, they buy into humanism after all.

The Vitruvian definition of architectural values leaves the door wide open for conflict, yet it remains the most durable. How best to cope with the ethical dimension of architecture has yet to be resolved by the leading architectural theorists. Does their failure in this regard portend that any account of the moral dimension of architecture is doomed to inconsistency? Is the fact that little agreement exists concerning the place of moral deliberation in design, or even the importance of architecture to the greater good, telling about the prospects for such agreement? Architectural theory has not explored these issues with the help of the perspectives moral philosophy can supply. The remainder of this book will address this void through a detailed examination of the values and moral dilemmas unique to architecture.

61

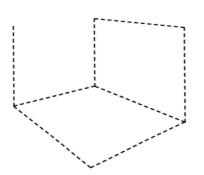

CHAPTER 3 | UTILITAS

Thousands of decisions go into the design of a moderately complex building, and many of these decisions require consideration of difficult trade-offs between desirable ends— ends that are irreconcilable within the context in which they are presented to the designer. In sorting through these decisions, architects carry on an internal debate regarding which ends are most important, which can be accommodated indirectly, and which need to be rejected so that a series of mutually reinforcing decisions can be made. For guidance, architects rely on their most deeply held values. This makes the work, in part at least, ethical.

At times, the conflicts appear so intractable that the designer concludes that the problem lies outside his or her control, in the givens of budget, schedule, site, or program. Amending the givens, however, is generally viewed as a last resort. Instead, architects often try to design their way out of tough situations, hoping that the results will either resolve most of the conflicts or prove so compelling that the trade-offs he or she was forced into making become invisible. Indeed, many architects and their clients think that this is the whole point of design. Designs that fail to surmount all difficulties generally reflect badly on the designer; either he or she simply did not try hard enough, or even worse, lacks talent.

For a designer to say that some design problems are simply intractable is to acknowledge defeat. Architects probably do not deserve to be held to such a high standard of ability, but they often subscribe to it themselves. Behind every mediocre building is an architect doubting his or her own talent and wondering whether someone else could have done it better. Self-doubt is a second order of inner debate architects engage in, and it, too, has ethical content.

In the absence of guiding principles, the inner debate architects engage in can become stymied and lead to contradictory or self-defeating actions. To avoid such undesirable results, it would be only natural to seek a way of comparing the relative benefits of possible design decisions. If a consistent standard against which to rank or compare designs were available, these obstacles to successful design synthesis could perhaps be avoided.[1]

Since the nineteenth century, much thought in this area has converged around the idea that competing, mutually exclusive design decisions should be measured against some notion of utility. The attraction of such an idea is manifold. Were a utilitarian measure possible, design decisions could be made less intuitively and more rationally. Hence, the discipline of architecture could experience the rapid progress characteristic of scientific disciplines. The benefits of design could be better appreciated by the public if those benefits were expressed in quantitative terms. In a world increasingly measured by calculations of all kinds—from corporate earnings to cost-benefit analyses to efficiency ratings—the vague benefits promised by the architect could better withstand the onslaught of more rationally justifiable goods and services.

The concept that utility is a crucial component of architecture has, of course, a distinguished provenance, beginning with Vitruvius' definition of architecture as providing

66

utilitas, firmitas, and *venustas.*[2] Moral philosophy also has a distinguished tradition, lodged in the concept of utilitarianism. This is not to say that moral utilitarianism and Vitruvian *utilitas* are precisely the same thing, but the two ideas have far greater similarities than differences.

The possibilities and problems of establishing a consistent standard of utility for evaluating design options come clearly into view when a single design decision is examined closely. The moral deliberations over the decision to preserve or tear down a cluster of apartments located in San Francisco's Presidio form the focus of this chapter and reveal the many facets of the concept of utility that may come to bear on one's decisions.

PROPOSITION L

The western approach to the Golden Gate Bridge is framed on the north by the rugged cliffs and isolated beaches of the Marin Headlands and on the south by a mile and a half of lush, coastal bluffs belonging to the Presidio of San Francisco. These elements frame a breathtaking view of the avenues and buildings of the city of San Francisco, cascading down steep hillsides to meet the bay's edge. In short, this is one of the most beautiful spots in the world.

The aesthetic effect of the Presidio would approach the perfection of Yosemite Valley or the Grand Canyon were it not marred by a 524-unit government-built eyesore named Wherry Housing. Perched on the cliffs above Baker Beach, the units are boxy, poorly detailed, employ cheap-looking materials, and are grouped in dense clusters that not even mature planting could obscure. Bringing Wherry Housing's appearance up to a level that might be called unobtrusive would be more costly than tearing the units down and building anew. As part of its plan to convert the Presidio from a military base to a national park, the

67

National Park Service hoped to demolish Wherry Housing. Saving the complex became such a *cause célèbre* that it became a local ballot initiative.

On June 2, 1998, San Franciscans were asked to vote on Proposition L, which stated,

> Shall the City and County of San Francisco, which has been asked to pay for and provide non-emergency support services to the Presidio, encourage the restoration of the land to natural open space, and act to ensure that the 1,900 existing housing units at the Presidio, including Wherry Housing, be preserved at the Presidio, with the majority of that existing housing to be set aside for rental to San Francisco residents of all income levels, including both affordable and market-rate housing?[3]

Most of the language contained in this proposition was a smoke-screen. The proposition attempted to do nothing about open space, and most of the other housing in the Presidio was already scheduled for reuse. This measure was primarily concerned with saving Wherry and apportioning a substantial number of units for rent at subsidized rates.[4] In a city with the worst housing affordability index in the nation, the thought of destroying Wherry and other housing projects on the grounds of the Presidio at a time when the demand for affordable housing would actually be on the increase due to the staffing needs of the newly created national park was anathema to the many citizens who struggled daily to help house those in need. Saving this housing would help the problem of providing adequate shelter to the city's citizens in a small but substantial way and would ease commuter-traffic problems in the neighborhoods around the Presidio. That mere aesthetics would cause the destruction of hundreds of housing units— buildings that could be brought up to code for a fraction of the cost of building from ground up—was considered outrageous

68

by many. Yet not even the proponents of the measure were bold enough to suggest that these buildings could ever be made to grace their location. Wherry Housing could only be placed back into service for the benefit of its lucky residents at the expense of the greater public's enjoyment of the Presidio National Park.

Spearheaded by the outspoken Sister Bernie Galvin, Proposition L garnered the support of a large number of religious and neighborhood groups, the Tenderloin Housing Clinic, the National Lawyers Guild, the San Francisco Green Party, the Senior Action Network, the Coalition on Homelessness, Habitat for Humanity, Dolores Street Community Services, the Mental Health Association, SF NOW PAC, the Campaign to Abolish Poverty, the Center for Ethics and Economic Policy, San Franciscans for Tax Justice, and many others. Those opposed to Proposition L included the Sierra Club, the San Francisco Planning and Urban Research Association, the Golden Gate National Recreation Advisory Commission, San Francisco Beautiful, and Congresswoman Nancy Pelosi.[5] Despite the fact that this debate concerned issues of abiding interest to architects, neither the AIA nor any other organized group of architects weighed in with an opinion. In that architects' opinions on these subjects are likely to be more thoughtful and sensitive than the average person's, it is sad that architects did not render an opinion. But what side should architects have taken in this debate?

MAXIMIZING THE GOOD

The philosophical doctrine of utilitarianism offers a simple and attractive answer to the problem facing San Franciscans: decide so as to maximize the good that will be brought about by your decision. With this moral directive, the problem of deciding over Proposition L becomes one of means, not of ends. The end—achieving the maximum good—has been predetermined. Theoretically, this should make the problem more manageable, more a matter of practical rationality than of moral deliberation. Determining which course of action maximizes the overall good can now take place by summing up the utilities offered by each and by choosing the one with the highest score. This approach has a further advantage; it is widely considered to be a reasonable and fair way of deciding. It appears reasonable because in everyday decision-making, the best result is invariably an important criterion. As philosopher Samuel Scheffler notes, the concept "seems hard to resist." He explains,

> For given only the innocent-sounding assumption that good is morally preferable to evil, it seems to embody the principle that we should maximize the desirable and minimize the undesirable, and that principle seems to be one of the main elements of our conception of practical rationality.[6]

Indeed, the National Park Service itself uses methods comparable to the philosophical doctrine of utilitarianism in its planning.[7]

What are the benefits, and the perils, if the National Park Service prevails and Wherry Housing is demolished? Tearing down the complex would do quite a bit of good for the San Francisco garter snake and other endangered species whose habitat is restricted to the Presidio. It would also provide some amount of good for the aesthetics of the Golden Gate and a small amount of good for each of the estimated three million yearly visitors by eliminating an impediment to their visual pleasure.

What if Proposition L's proponents prevail and Wherry Housing is preserved? On the scale of ecological good and aesthetic pleasure, saving Wherry would do a modest amount

70

of good for the neighborhoods surrounding the Presidio by reducing the number of national parks employees commuting on their streets. It would also do quite a bit of good for some families in need of housing and a small amount of good for San Franciscans in general by adding to and improving the city's housing stock. From the perspective of improving a pressing problem of the human condition, supporting Proposition L is almost certainly the better choice.

Adherents to the doctrine of utilitarianism would have us look beyond our personal preferences and predilections in determining which option would result in the "most overall utility." What is meant by the phrase "most overall utility?" For John Stuart Mill, this meant human happiness.[8] This measure of utility, however, has gone into decline. More up-to-date contenders include personal preference, desire, the right to pursue one's own interests, social welfare, "the equal interests of everybody," and even the urge to minimize inequalities in distribution of goods throughout the world.[9] In the case of indecision, the utilitarian would choose the option "whose effects have at least as great a utility-sum as the effects of any other option."[10]

In order to calculate the maximum good, the preferences of everyone affected by the decision must be evaluated from an impartial standpoint. Examining the sum total of utilities due everyone with something at stake in the decision would allow us to determine which option is best, preserving Wherry or tearing it down. A preliminary decision must be made regarding what sort of preferences to include in one's deliberations; do we, for instance, accept a plebiscite by those affected by our decisions, or do we, as R. M. Hare recommends, consider "the desires of others, considering what they would be if those others were perfectly prudent—i.e. desired what they would desire if they were fully informed and unconfused."[11] Hare argues that a

71

simple canvassing is unacceptable because people are notoriously ill-informed and shortsighted in their decision-making, so one must inform oneself as best one can and act according to what seems to be in everyone's long-term best interests. Architects' superior knowledge in design matters would make them ideally suited to determine people's preferences in this instance.

Several warning flags should go up at Hare's statement. First, if we accept the view that it is appropriate and even desirable for architects to have a value system that is slightly at variance with the general population's, then shouldn't architects consult those values, rather than society's, in their design deliberations?[12] If an architect deliberates using what he or she thinks society's values should be were people more prudent, a disjunction is implied. An architect's values are justifiably more partisan, informed by professional considerations and expertise. If an architect is charged with consulting his or her personal values, then no claim can be made for universalizing his or her design thinking, and hence, acting according to what would maximize the good. Only a tyrant can maintain that his personal values are the public's. If an architect seeks to avoid this problem by consulting the preferences of people as they are given, rather than as they would be if people were more prudent, then one is abdicating one's role and discarding one's superior knowledge. Hare thinks this problem can be avoided by simply placing oneself in the other's position.[13]

Utilitarians think that this course of action will resolve conflicts of values, but it will not. We adhere to different (and incompatible) outlooks that would prevent this role-taking. As an architect, one would value beauty; as a homeless advocate, one would value housing. How is role-taking supposed to help this situation? In the case of Proposition L, utilitarianism would seem to resolve the problem far too quickly. It becomes pointless to give the opposition's point of view deep thought, because the situation is a true toss-up. Therefore, the decision turns on a matter of popularity, and the ethical choice becomes whichever one receives the most votes. Although this may be an acceptable means for resolving ethical disputes, it makes a peculiar substitute for ethical judgment. Popularity contests can only bear a glancing resemblance to moral decision-making. In toss-up situations, the decision-maker is actually prevented by utilitarianism (at least Hare's version) from being as morally sensitive as he or she would like to be.

This would seem to be an impossible situation. A practitioner can either deliberate as an architect or deliberate universally, but he or she cannot do both simultaneously. Even if the architect's value system did not differ from that of those affected by his or her decisions, considering what people ought to think, rather than what they do think, smacks of paternalism. One can ultimately justify any bias on the basis of what people *ought* to think, and nothing in the concept of prudential preferences can prevent this.

More immediate to the problem at hand, one can universalize what people would prefer from the perspectives of everyone affected and still remain unconvinced of a clear decision at the Presidio. When a large benefit for a few is pitted against a small benefit for many, which utility-sum is greater? Rephrasing the deliberation to consider, instead of preferences, the sum of the expected utilities creates a similar problem. It is still unclear which side would win out.

Utilitarians tend to downplay this as a problem. Utilitarian philosopher John Harsanyi argues that "careful analysis will almost invariably show that the most important source of moral and political disagreements among people of goodwill

73

lies in divergent judgments about future development and about the future consequences of alternative policies."[14] Frequently people have a good idea about who will benefit and who will suffer as the result of a design decision. They also know what those benefits, and disutilities, will be. Regarding Proposition L, it is not too difficult to determine the factors to be compared.

On the housing side, we can estimate that over twenty years approximately four thousand people will live in Wherry Housing for some period of time and that their lives will be significantly enhanced. On the aesthetics side, there will be approximately sixty million visits enhanced a little bit over twenty years. We should also include some utility for the endangered species that will benefit should the tear-down option prevail. People of goodwill on both sides can agree on these effects, but disagree on the value of these effects. In this case, we have come no further. The utilitarian demand for universalizing one's opinions has gone unfulfilled. What is lacking is not a means for determining outcomes, but a common moral currency against which outcomes can be measured.

COVERING VALUES

If it turns out that "the most overall utility" depends upon which set of equally plausible and apparently rational values one subscribes to, then the possibility presents itself that one may be able to rank, not the outcomes, but the sets of values appealed to by these outcomes. The decision has been "kicked upstairs," so to speak, to a higher level of abstraction. These two sets of values, however, can only be ranked against a third, what Ruth Chang calls a "covering value."[15] That is, they can only be rated against a value that both these sets of values have in common.

Several candidates for "covering value" come to mind in the case of Proposition L. First, one might consider which is harder to come by, aesthetic perfection or decent housing. The scarcity of one or the other might increase its value and tip the scales in its favor. Decent housing might be built elsewhere in the city, but there is only one place for the Presidio and only one Golden Gate Bridge. So, if scarcity is considered an important value, then opposing Proposition L maximizes the good.

Or perhaps one would invoke adherence to the traditional purpose of the National Park System to guide the decision. If this is deemed a relevant criterion, then opposing Proposition L would again emerge as the best choice. Some believe, however, that the standards of the National Park System are in need of updating. They would like the Park Service to include decent housing within its parks. These critics of the current system would find good reason to support Proposition L.

One might measure the choices on Proposition L against the value which requires the least commitment to permanent change. Given the unequivocal nature of the values embodied in the choices, simply choosing the one that precludes the least amount of subsequent alternatives might be of value. If this consideration is allowed to rule, saving Wherry Housing is clearly the best alternative. It can always be torn down later, but it is highly unlikely that it could ever be rebuilt once destroyed.

Finally, one might recognize that both saving and destroying Wherry Housing have plenty of merit and that the best thing to do is to decide which choice is most deserving according to the principle of taking turns. In this particular case, however, taking turns is an unclear concept. Taking turns in what regard? If taking turns refers to land use, then perhaps it is time to return the land to its natural state. If taking turns refers to concepts for administering a national park, then preserving Wherry Housing would be best. Similarly, for such

75

over-arching concepts as improving the social good of the nation, enhancing democratic institutions, or insuring the greatest good for the greatest number, it is unclear which set of values provides the best fit.

Others have advanced the idea that basing one's choice on the greatest good generated by the alternative is irrelevant in this case. They think that the proposition itself endangers already shaky Congressional support for the costly endeavor of transforming the Presidio into a national park.[16] The funding for the whole project risks being withdrawn by Congress if San Franciscans try to force their influence. This argument seeks to trump any consideration of the value of the alternatives presented by Proposition L by raising the possibility of a much worse—even catastrophic—consequence. This move attempts to take the consideration of the greatest good out of the actual merits of the alternatives presented by Proposition L and place the decision on the question, "should I or shouldn't I take this as a proper topic of deliberation?" It unleashes a fresh set of issues to worry over, such as whether power politics make this an improper area of deliberation.

The initial merits of each alternative begin to recede in prominence, as all sorts of possible covering values crowd the decision-making process, adding to the amount of material that must be weighed to determine the best choice or trumping the rest of the goods with one single good—the "sacred value," in Steven Lukes' terms, that must not be ignored.[17] The susceptibility of regressing from the actual problem at hand is one of the characteristic problems of this way of thinking.[18] Casting too small a net around what one is willing to consider results in deliberations that can no longer be called maximizing. Casting too wide a net in one's deliberations results in vague criteria and in less and less confidence in their results.

THE ETHICAL ARCHITECT

Some design critics charge that the problem is not with the plurality of values or vagueness of ends represented by different design solutions, but in the plurality of methods used to evaluate them. These people believe that design needs to be more systematic to avoid this endless regress of considerations and the proliferation of values less relevant to the problem at hand. They think that a certain fuzzy-headedness regarding decisions with an artistic or social dimension infects one's deliberations, a fuzziness that needs to be cleared away. A defined set of processes would make up for the lack of a clearly related set of ends. This attitude has a basis in utilitarianism.

All process-oriented design methods have in common the concept that a set of criteria is developed against which the design is scored.[19] The overall evaluation consists of a bundle of partial evaluations. Each partial evaluation is given a value, a percentage of the whole. The design alternative that receives the highest score wins. This technique substitutes a bunch of smaller intuitive decisions for one large one. Presumed in this method is the idea that, while an overall evaluation of a building design may be too complex to be transparent, a bunch of smaller intuitions is open to outside evaluation and critique. No limit is set on the number of criteria one may choose, and each possible design decision is measured against all the criteria. The scoring can be simple or sophisticated. One may, for instance, take a weighted average for some criteria, while for other criteria the lowest score may rule.

In the case of Proposition L, voting to tear down Wherry would receive a zero score under the criterion of providing living space, while voting to save Wherry would receive an equally low score on aesthetic value. Choosing a winner

77

becomes largely a matter of deciding which partial evaluation criterion one holds to be the most dear—in this case, housing or aesthetics.

The synthetic method substitutes the assertion made earlier, that the two choices can only be assessed according to different criteria, with a second assertion, that if a solution simply does not respond to a certain criterion, then it deserves a low score. There simply is no category for "not applicable." Although the assertion that irrelevance or non-responsiveness equals a zero score strikes some critics as problematic, this is not the only problem posed by this method. From a moral point of view, two other problems arise; first, that it treats the criteria as givens, and second, that it treats goodness as a finite number. Determining that saving Wherry Housing measures poorly against aesthetics is a shallow achievement, one that ultimately adds little to one's understanding of the choices. We could come up with any number of hitherto irrelevant, or "not applicable," considerations that would serve to lower our estimation of one option or the other. Yet weighted average systems would have us make such a determination and hold it up as significant. The problem with the methodological approach is obvious. The real work of one's decision-making has already been done, by deciding that improved human habitation is a relevant criterion. Once this decision is made, the final choice on Proposition L is inevitable.

This conclusion, however, brings up an important distinction between a single design decision and designing. Choosing between options is only one crucial step in the process. Proposition L requires a design decision, but isolates this decision from the larger and more complex act of designing. This important distinction must be made between designing and the weighted-average system as well. Deciding

78

which criteria should be employed is not part of the evaluation procedure. A method for making these decisions may well exist, but it is not modeled here. The system is silent on the ethical business of deciding what the appropriate values are. Perhaps the basis for deciding is intuition, or perhaps the values simply reflect preference. Perhaps these preferences are supposed to reflect a well-established and thoroughly argued set of beliefs. Even if the basis for deciding on the appropriate values is the latter, none of these supports is enough to overcome the problem of the system which skews the results.

Weighted-average techniques attempt to make design evaluations more transparent, but they do so at the expense of forcing us to give certain judgments an importance that we would not give them in ordinary deliberation. The weighted-average technique works well to explain our preferences when the options under consideration are similar. When two designs are under consideration, alike except that one has a fire sprinkler system and the other has a firewall separation system, then the evaluation method does little to skew the processes of ordinary deliberation. But then neither does it tell us much we couldn't figure out using less formal methods.

As this illustration shows, weighted-average systems are not helpful in decisions where conflicting values operate because they become problematic as soon as they substitute quantitative information for qualitative. As Ruth Chang puts it, the question posed to practical reason is not necessarily, "How much better?" but "In what way better?" or "To what extent better?"[20] These qualitative questions more closely match those designers ask themselves than do the quantitative one. More sophisticated and rigorous decision-making processes will be of no help either. The problem of deciding for or against Proposition L does not lie with the process. We are no closer to reaching a decision than before. To those who would say that, regardless of our qualms about measuring the aesthetics of the Presidio against San Francisco's pressing housing shortage, we are actually doing so anyway when we enter the voting booth, we may politely reply, "not so." We may be attempting to do that, but we are doing something else. When one tries to model the claim that such things are not really incommensurable, no helpful model of commensuration emerges. Applying the weighted-average method demonstrates that all we find are circular arguments based on preference, a skewed vision of what is actually going on, or a model that can only handle the easy problems.

INCOMMENSURABLES

Treating the situation at the Presidio as a conflict of incommensurable values avoids these problems. Accepting that the values represented by the choices on Proposition L are conflicting and incommensurable does not, however, mean that nothing meaningful can be said to help the undecided voter, nor that the process is irrational. As Bernard Williams, John Dewey, Michael Stocker, Elizabeth Anderson, and others point out, deciding between incommensurables is hardly an exceptional undertaking; rather, it is an everyday business. An architectural design decision differs from the everyday in the durability and far-reaching nature of its consequences. The stakes are high enough to warrant pursuing some way to rationally evaluate the choice between incommensurables.

Philosophers discuss incommensurables quite a lot these days: what they are, where they come from, how to know one when you see one, and even whether they really exist. Some see incommensurability as the inevitable result of curbing human appetites for the benefits of socialization.[21] Others see

80

it as the result of values learned and transmitted over time in social situations—values that, due to the contingency of such processes, are inevitably conflicting.[22] Another group sees the plurality of incommensurables to be the very foundation of the Western, liberal way of life.[23] Yet another train of thought regards value pluralism as emanating from the many ways we have of caring about things.[24] Still another sees moral conflict to be inevitable due to the fact that no moral theory completely determines what to do in every situation.[25] Arguing for or against any of these points of view, or for that matter, the existence or nonexistence of moral dilemmas is unnecessary to make the point that regarding difficult trade-offs in design decisions as commensurable leads to ways of thinking that are foreign to design. Of course tearing down Wherry rates poorly on the affordable housing scale. Of course saving this eyesore rates poorly on the aesthetic scale. Only by regarding these options as incommensurable and looking elsewhere for good reasons for action can we hope to break out of this unhelpful way of evaluating the decision.

INTENTIONS AND DESIRES

Some critics think that one's intentions and motivations count for a great deal and that the importance of intentions should be somehow accounted for in moral delineations. They observe that architectural designers, when they sit down at the drafting table, intend to maximize the good. If it becomes impossible to determine which course of action will achieve the best outcome, then designers want to make their decisions according to good reasons. Treating conflicting design options as incommensurable defeats this motivation. This objection contains two good points. The first is that intentions matter a great deal. The second point is that designers seek good

81

reasons to back up what they do. Indeed, "lack of good reasons" is often cited as one of the hallmarks of incommensurability.[26] Filling this void stands to eliminate moral conflict.

What does the "good reasons" objection achieve? It can only be true that a lack of good reasons exists and also be true that the design decision can still be a subject of practical deliberation if the lack of good reasons refers not to reasons to like an alternative, but to reasons to rank one alternative above another. For if no good reason exists to even like an alternative to begin with, then certainly no good reason exists to place it in contention with other possible choices. Regardless of how strongly motivated he or she is, a designer may well seek and find good reasons to like certain alternatives, but still be no farther down the road of decision-making. This seems to be the case with Proposition L; good reasons to tilt for one side or the other abound, but at the end of the day, the values represented by the choices are still incommensurable.

Philosopher Joseph Raz thinks that, in the void left by the lack of sufficient reasons focused on the relative merits of each possible action, our wants will be ushered in to help make the decision: "A want can never tip the balance of reasons in and of itself. Rather, our wants become relevant when reasons have run their course . . . once reason has failed to adjudicate between a range of options, we normally choose one for no further reason, simply because we want to."[27] This doesn't preclude having reasons to back up wants but it does imply that these wants are not directly the result of rational deliberation. The wants he refers to must have existed prior to consideration of this design decision, otherwise these wants would be generated by the merits and demerits of the options under consideration, and hence there would have been no incommensurability in the first place. An egoistic outlook is allowed to rule in the absence of a definitive moral reason.

Personal preference tips the balance. Raz maintains that the actor remains within the bounds of morality, because consideration of duty or virtue or of whatever values one holds to be relevant is given first crack.

The designer who relies on wants is now exercising his decision-making power for his own benefit and no longer for reasons we would take to have moral content. He justifies this by reasoning that since either course of action is good enough, he can really do no wrong, regardless of the choice he makes.

Designers who would like to purge morality from design would be heartened by this development, because it justifies pursuing one's own wants. Why bother with all this discussion of morality if it turns out that most of the time the decision will turn on one's personal preferences anyway? The morally motivated design professional, on the other hand, will have a problem with this conclusion and would wonder with good reason if those on the losing side in the decision would find such reasoning as consoling as would those on the winning side.

Raz does not mean to take his observations this far. He only seeks to show that the entry of wants into deliberations is not inconsistent with practical reason. He finds that "ordinary human experience . . . teaches us that quite commonly people do not survey all the options open to them before choosing what to do. Rather, they find an option that they believe not to be excluded by reason and that appeals to them and pursue it."[28] This does not mean, however, that the designer is not making his decisions out of raw aggression. Just because an option is acceptable according to good reasons does not make choosing that option anything more than an exercise of one's will, unless reasons for rejecting other acceptable options that are related to those options are put forth. The fact that people make decisions before all possible options are consulted says more about the practical impossibility of canvassing all options than

83

it does about the moral acceptability of exercising one's power of choice. One may be prevented, as designers frequently are, from looking at all plausible options due to time constraints, for instance, or lack of experience, but these are good reasons about the problem of too many options, not about one's wants. Simply requiring that the options first pass a threshold of acceptability before a single option is selected based on want does not insulate the designer from the charge of egoism.

There is an alternative, however, to embracing egoism when faced with incommensurable design options. If the desires an architect references in making design decisions are the right kind, then the exercise of his or her will in those might fall within an ethical framework. Elizabeth Anderson calls these "right-kind" of desires one's ideals:

> Ideals are objects, not merely of desire, but of aspiration. Ideals give us perspectives from which to articulate and scrutinize the ways we value things. The core of an ideal consists in a conception of qualities of character, or characteristics of the community, which the holders regard as excellent and as central to their identities. Associated with this core is a conception of admirable conduct or worthy practices and projects that demand the cultivation, exercise, and expression of these qualities.[29]

Instead of an architect trying to decide between options from a neutral stance, his or her self-conception would play an important part in the deliberations. Anderson terms this the expressive theory of value.

Expressive theory has three things going for it that could help the designer find the good reasons needed to make difficult decisions. First, it does not rely on commensurability to make comparisons between alternative courses of action. Treating values as plural is expected, although perhaps still a complicating factor for decision-making. Second, it acknowledges—even champions—the subjectivity that bedevils attempts to evaluate one's options objectively. Third, it recognizes the importance of one's intentions in deciding which course of action to pursue, thus providing a richer interpretation of right and wrong, good and bad, than does the concept of maximizing overall utility.

What is the place of one's intentions in an overall evaluation of a design decision? The morally motivated designer would want to be able to care about the option not chosen, as well as the one chosen. He would want his decision to reflect his compassion and kindness. Making a choice among the available options would be influenced by considering which one would best allow him to be the sort of person he wishes to be and to act in ways he feels most comfortable. He would want these intentions to correspond with considerations of maximizing the good.

Is a concern for intentions consistent with a utilitarian outlook, or is it inimicable to utility? Anderson would have us believe that expressive theory excludes a strictly utilitarian orientation, but the utilitarian is unlikely to be so easily convinced. Expressive theory and the utilitarian outlook share a common concern for the welfare of mankind. They both champion individual responsibility for taking moral action. Where they differ is that utilitarians would judge all decisions against a single good, whereas proponents of expressive theory would hold no opinion on this subject. This difference may not be insurmountable; value pluralism is expected by expressive theory, if not required.

What might cause more severe conflict between the two outlooks is that utilitarianism requires the moral agent to

85

regard actions from an impartial point of view, and expressive theory requires agents to deliberate from a particular one. This is the crucial difference that stands to lead to different styles of deliberating and to different outcomes. As an advocate for the homeless, an architect might support Proposition L. Expressive theory would require nothing less. Utilitarianism requires us to check our various self-interests at the door in favor of considering what would be best for everyone. For those architects who identify themselves as social activists, rather than aesthetes, the choice would again be clear. Yet, architects must also identify themselves by some common characteristic, or else the identity of "architect" would be empty. One could be considered a good architect without being a social activist, but it is doubtful whether one could be considered a good architect without being deeply concerned with aesthetics. According to expressive theory, then, the mainstream of the profession is most likely to think that opposing Proposition L gets at more of its basic self-definition, despite the fact that there would be a faction of architects who think otherwise.

Expressive theory shifts the focus away from an impartial examination of the features of the case to a highly particular examination of the relationship between one's self-definition and the decision at hand. Utilitarians will despair at the loss of universality inherent in such a turn. The utilitarian hope for a world community has been replaced by a vision of a population of competing individual and group values. An important element, however, has been preserved; expressive theory allows an ethical concern to carry all the way through the decision-making process and it does so without requiring the decision-maker to become so abstract in his or her reasoning that he or she becomes removed from the problem at hand.

UTILITAS

The attempt by modernists and other architectural theorists to make the Vitruvian notion of *utilitas* into the overarching value against which all architectural goods are measured suffers from the same problem that afflicts philosophical utilitarianism when applied to design decisions. Demanding that all the goods provided by design be comparable and ranked against a concept of utility disregards the importance of a distinctly architectural outlook. It either leads us to looking farther and farther afield to find a common measure against which to judge alternatives, or it encourages us to judge alternatives against standards they were never meant to address. By holding to the pluralism of values implied by the Vitruvian triumvirate, architects need not rely exclusively on the probability of different outcomes to inform their design decisions.

Unlike an all-inclusive utilitarianism, *utilitas* has traditionally implied a specific and finite set of goals: that a building's design should support certain well-defined functions. Making utility into something more overarching and abstract may well have stretched the concept past the breaking point. Whether nineteenth- and twentieth-century attempts to enlarge this concept have increased or decreased the architect's ability to deliberate using practical rationality would make for an interesting debate. Enlarging the traditional role of *utilitas* in design deliberation has at best put off the dilemmas of design and at worst papered-over them. Vitruvius clearly recognized the possibility of conflicts in values, but maintained that they were easily resolved by the "good architect." He makes the resolution of these conflicts a matter of both expertise and character.

Architects may lament the apparent loss of practical rationality in discarding a monist doctrine like utilitarianism. The example of the design decision to be made here suggests that treating utility as a superior value is a concept better left behind. There is nothing inherently irrational about value pluralism, simply because it acknowledges that unranked qualities of various goods cannot be expressed as rankable quantities without the loss of something important. This inability to rank need not lead to inaction, nor to anguish over the possibility of making the less-than-optimum choice. As Amartya Sen and Bernard Williams observed,

> To be unable to rank may be frustrating, but by itself it could scarcely be a failure of rationality. To insist, following the lead of "revealed preference" theory, that rational choice requires that x can be chosen when y is available only if—everything considered—x is regarded as at least as good as y, imposes a peculiar limitation on choice. The real "irrationality" of Buridan's ass rested not in its inability to rank the two haystacks, but in its refusal to choose either haystack without being perfectly sure that that haystack was better than, or at least as good as, the other (surely an asinine attempt to be faithful to an odd theory of "rational choice"). It can be argued that rational choice based on an incomplete ordering requires only that a not inferior alternative be picked. This would have required Buridan's ass to pick either haystack, but not *neither*, which was clearly an inferior alternative.[30]

In the end, Proposition L passed and Wherry Housing has been reinstated to active duty over the National Park Service's objections. Rather than help influence this important design decision, the architectural profession only looked on. This missed opportunity may not have been the direct result of a utilitarian paralysis, but neither has a pervasive utilitarian outlook made us any more prepared to act the next time a design issue takes the public stage.

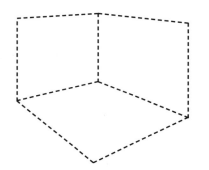

CHAPTER 4 | VENUSTAS

Convention-shattering designs are lionized in the architectural press for the breakthrough ideas and aesthetic novelties they embody, and justly so. This fascination with the unconventional, however, tends to champion risk-taking work without ever really examining what's at stake in taking such risks. As long as risk-taking is confined to the aesthetic realm, a work does not pose undue challenges to interpretation and judgment; designs that also conform to customary functional requirements do not call for a theory that relates the aesthetic and the moral. But what of other situations, in which aesthetic decisions result in a significant challenge to conventional expectations of a building's utility?

The history of modern architecture is rife with aesthetic experiments that made for uncomfortable living, never worked as promised, or weathered poorly. This list includes such well-known works as Mies van der Rohe's Farnsworth House in Plano, Illinois, Louis Kahn's Richards Medical Research Center in Philadelphia, and perhaps the most famous of all, Frank Lloyd Wright's Guggenheim Museum in New York. In these works, a tension between the use value and aesthetic value of the building has long been acknowledged. In hailing works like the Guggenheim aesthetic masterpieces, we are encouraged to discount the very real hardships that they caused their users. Maintaining such an outlook has implications for the work designed by today's architects. By exploring the problems that the Guggenheim poses for interpretation and judgment, we stand to better determine the value that *venustas* plays in contemporary design.

The functional problems of Wright's Guggenheim were obvious from the start. Although it created a thrilling sense of vertical space, the museum's spiral ramp made for difficulties in viewing works of art. Paintings appeared to be hung askew to the floor plane and lacked proper lighting. Even Lewis Mumford, usually a champion of Wright's work, observed that at the Guggenheim, Wright "succumbed to the fascination of an elegant mechanical solution, treated as an end in itself."[1]

Design decisions that were motivated by aesthetic concerns at the Guggenheim negatively impact the central functioning of Wright's building. We are speaking of nothing so minor as a leaky roof or some hard-to-clean surfaces. The functional problems brought on by the design's aesthetic are sufficiently severe as to militate against unreserved admiration of the building as a whole. That we could admire this building aesthetically, however, in spite of the fact that its aesthetics directly diminish its use value, is not the problem to be reckoned with here; there is nothing especially unusual in concluding, "it's beautiful, but unworkable." How we might choose to reconcile an unfavorable functional judgment with a favorable aesthetic one forms the question to be explored.

The Guggenheim is unique, if not in the fact that its use and aesthetic values conflict, then in the degree of its aesthetic success. Had it been an aesthetically ordinary building, the value conflict between aesthetics and utility would have been easily resolved in favor of a negative overall assessment.

Buildings frequently have defects that are the direct result of their virtues. Lightweight, flexible buildings require increased maintenance. Extremely tight, energy-efficient buildings experience problems in maintaining acceptable air quality. Highly contextual buildings ingratiate too completely with their context, while the heroic or original buildings fail to fit comfortably into theirs. The difference between the Guggenheim and less celebrated buildings is only the degree to which it is admired aesthetically. How one reconciles these conflicting judgments is highly dependent on the degree to which one values aesthetic goods, as a component of a person's overall moral outlook. The tendency to admire such buildings in the face of such well-known failures may inform, as well as reflect, one's ethics.

Three strategies for reconciling aesthetic and moral values may be observed. One could start with the aesthete's conception of value and ascribe a moral dimension to it. One might also begin from a moral outlook and attempt to carve out a uniquely aesthetic component. Or one might start from a pluralist outlook, which regards both the aesthetic and ethical values as irreducible and complementary components of architectural judgment.

THE AESTHETE

The aesthete judges architecture to be centrally about the aesthetic of building. Functional considerations are thought to be secondary and tend to enter into one's critical thinking only to the degree that they positively or negatively impact aesthetic judgment. The aesthete gives weight to the observation that a building's aesthetic value is generally long-term, while use-value can be startlingly mercurial. This observation allows the aesthete to conclude that aesthetic value trumps utility.

The aesthete's focus may cause him or her to appear inherently cavalier, but this is not necessarily the case. The aesthete may be a highly moral person with a relatively compartmentalized outlook about the legitimate place of moral thinking. He or she may simply believe that the primary aim of the architect is to make buildings beautiful and that bringing utility into the discussion poisons the pot. Such a view may have a legitimate point. Lots of issues relevant to architecture are extraneous to issues of aesthetics. We should not have to be distracted by whether the building is profitable, or has a persistent roof leak, or is made from steel that comes from a nation engaged in unfair dumping practices when considering it aesthetically, unless these conditions intrude upon our ability to do so. This ability to mentally compartmentalize the issues makes sense of our tendency to admire the Guggenheim despite its functional failures.

How does the aesthete justify his or her persistent valuing of aesthetics in the face of more pressing concerns? The aesthete either needs a concept of aesthetics that includes moral value, or needs to be willing to do without a claim to relevance of the larger scheme of things.

Aesthetic theory contributes a number of concepts that attempt to explain aesthetic value. The creation and consumption of aesthetic goods has been argued to be a form of communication, therapy, expression, hedonism, cognition, a form of knowledge; it has been called a necessary ingredient to a moral outlook and the backbone of cultural development, among other things.[2] The theories associated with these arguments, however, justify aesthetic value instrumentally. Such justification does not seem to capture the reason people engage in aesthetic activity. Most do so for its own sake, as one of the goods.

Aesthetic experience may be one of life's goods, but the aesthete is hard-pressed for a concept of how to compare it to other goods. Philosopher Richard Miller identifies this as a problem when he writes,

> Any plausible rationale for taking aesthetic value to be a deeply important aspect of life must somehow connect it with our striving for knowledge or virtue. Yet such a rationale for the importance of art threatens to trivialize art in another way, by making the importance of art depend on its usefulness as an aid to nonaesthetic values. If serious aesthetic value is a substantial response to needs that intellectual and moral inquiry must create and must thwart, then it is appropriately connected to truth and virtue yet not subordinated to them.[3]

In ordinary circumstances, the aesthete need not justify the high regard he or she places on aesthetic experience, but when such justification is required, he or she cannot supply it without resorting to moral justifications. The aesthete's compartmentalization of the aesthetic and the moral may not be so stable after all.

THE STRICT MORALIST

At the opposite end of the spectrum is the strict moralist, who would be skeptical that a well-rounded, ethical person could come away with a positive assessment of buildings like the Guggenheim in the face of such obvious functional shortcomings. Sharing the belief expressed by Stuart Hampshire, that "There are no problems of aesthetics comparable with the problem of ethics,"[4] the strict moralist would claim that those who experience a tug between aesthetic values and other human goods are effete and out-of-touch with the values of society. The strict moralist subordinates the aesthetic to the moral, and he or she allows the aesthete to continue his or her practices without interfering only so long as those practices do not impinge on the moral. Admirers of the Guggenheim, according to this view, would ultimately be forced to acknowledge the building's failure due to its functional shortcomings.

This is not to equate the strict moralist with the functionalist. The strict moralist may well have other criteria in mind in addition or in place of utility. It would, however, be an extreme position to claim moral motivation and not share the functionalist's value of, say, comfort or security, which buildings are supposed to provide. More likely, the strict moralist would place a high degree of importance on functional concerns, but would not value these exclusively.

Although the strict moralist may be better equipped than the aesthete to articulate his position, his outlook is not necessarily more convincing. Architects in particular may share Friedrich Nietzsche's suspicion that the moralist's position is only an excuse for timidity in action.[5] Practitioners often despair about constraints imposed in the name of the common, moral good—design regulations, public concerns, demands for contextual sensitivity, and the like—that only serve to tame a strong design concept into something too nice to be interesting.[6] They see a conflict between artistic excellence and moral good. We might, for example, say that a building meets user needs, is contextually appropriate, and gentle to the environment, and yet still be reserved in our praise. It is too nice—all genuflection, when what is required is a certain amount of assertiveness. This circumstance is exactly what Nietzsche found so distasteful. He expressed disgust with philosophers who view congeniality as though it were the highest aim of humanity.[7]

Certainly, morality calls for self-restraint on occasion, but summoning self-restraint may require a tremendous exertion of will and require us to find the strongest and best within ourselves. At other times, a concern for morality may require us to take an active role in influencing events—the opposite of timidity. What Nietzsche refers to as "morality as timidity" is not timidity of will, but a dilution of some valuable, if less congenial, goods of life for morality's sake, resulting in a life of mild-manners and tamed passions. Art is generally thought to be one of the goods that knows nothing about congeniality. Architects all too often find themselves advancing art's cause against the morality of timidity.

Is Nietzsche's suspicion justified? Must a concern for morality in architecture lead to a watered-down artistic vision? At first blush, the answer appears to be "yes." Art, which needs autonomy to flourish, can only be diminished by the demands of utility. Such thinking led Adolph Loos to hold up that most useless of building types, the funeral monument, as one of the few works of pure architecture.[8]

Concerns for the well-being of each person affected by a building will undoubtedly take away time and effort that could otherwise be devoted to artistry. If the architect lacks fortitude, his or her vision will be crushed by accommodating concerns about a building's effects on its inhabitants, neighbors, community, and environment. In this context, we can appreciate the innovative offer by modernism's proponents to eliminate this old antagonism between beauty and use by deriving the former directly from the latter. The modernist approach performs a rather nice judo-flip on the moralist's claim of foundational superiority. Its seductive offer to "have it all" is, as Karsten Harries argues, a worthy notion.[9] As it actually played out, however, modernists all too often either tortured function for aesthetic ends or

97

demanded function from features that were the exclusive province of beauty.

THE PLURALIST

The pluralist seeks a reconciliation between the moralist and the aesthete by arguing that aesthetic concerns are conceptually on par with the functional, but that a lack in fulfilling either value must ultimately result in a negative assessment of the building under consideration. This position grants equal weight to both aesthetic and use values in matters of architectural judgment; neither is considered to be strong enough to carry the day alone.

The pluralist's position is more closely aligned than either the aesthete's or the strict moralist's with the position traditionally espoused by architects. The stability of such a view, however, might be questioned. By asserting the necessity of both the aesthetic and the functional, does it make adequate room for the exceptional? What becomes of the Pyramids, the Tempietto, or the Barcelona Pavilion, which lack the requisite functional agenda by this accounting? Holding these structures to functional standards would result in a negative assessment.

Perhaps the pluralist's outlook could be amended to maintain,

> Both functional and aesthetic agendas must be considered.
>
> If no functional agenda exists, it is acceptable to consider the aesthetic agenda alone.
>
> In any event, an aesthetic agenda must always be present.

Does this make the necessary adjustment or does this perhaps resolve the problem too easily?

Without the mandate that these competing values be somehow reconciled, we become engaged in architectural relativism. The Guggenheim may be fine for you, but not for me. The person who would claim that the functional agenda of the Guggenheim Museum was so trivial as to count for little in an overall evaluation of the building would be denying the very importance of a functional agenda. The amended outlook opens the door to this development, because it makes the question of the relevance of a functional agenda part of the deliberation, rather than one of the givens. It compels the observer to meditate on the very relevance of function in this instance.

Other issues become difficult to resolve under the pluralistic view. How, for instance, does a person make a stable distinction between architecture and sculpture, or between architecture and landscape design, or between architecture and engineering, if the requirement of reconciling aesthetics and utility is dropped from architectural judgment? The fact that disciplinary distinctions are blurred may well attest to the idea that, in practice, these fields are not as separate as their categorization suggests. This would be a boon to the pluralist view, as long as this view does not also suggest that each discipline's unique knowledge base and outlook do not exist.

Does the modified statement provide the conceptual tool needed to make a cut between architecture and sculpture, or landscape, or engineering? Architects, perhaps, do not really want to make this cut. They want to be able to include the great engineering form-givers Joseph Paxton, Pier Luigi Nervi, and John A. Roebling in their pantheon of great architects. They are moved by the architectural characteristics in the landscapes of Lawrence Halprin. They think it sensible to see Michelangelo the sculptor and Michelangelo the architect as a single figure. Although the pluralist can insist on the interrelatedness of disciplines, when required finally to impose

99

standards and make distinctions between architecture and non-architecture, his or her outlook seems to founder in ways the moralist's and the aesthete's do not. Neither the moralist nor the aesthete has much riding on a definition of architecture. They derive the normative basis of their judgments from beliefs about priorities. The pluralist has eschewed prioritizing in matters of conflict between aesthetics and function, but must hang his or her hat on something. That something, it turns out, must either be a clear-cut definition of what architecture provides (i.e., buildings with both function and beauty), or acceptance of relativism in normative judgments of both architectural merit and the distinction between architecture and non-architecture. If the pluralist does not wish to adhere to a strict definition of what architecture provides, because it would require him or her to marginalize otherwise important works, then relativism cripples him or her in asserting a preference for one work over another.

In recent times, the substitute of choice for the pluralist's problem of defining just what constitutes a work of architecture has been filled by institutional theory, which substitutes disciplinary solidarity for definitional objectivity. A work of architecture, according to this view, is what people within the discipline say it is. Thus, one no longer has to worry over whether the Tempietto will fall out of one's definition of architecture, so long as the majority of important people in the discipline agree that it is part of a relevant tradition. Pluralists can now maintain that aesthetics and function have equal importance. They need not resort to prioritizing between the two values of beauty and use, nor must they adhere to a rigid definition of architecture to have a means for making judgments, because their outlook is now bolstered by the institutional theory that states that architectural judgment, in both the objective and normative senses, is a matter of consensus.

However cleverly it may address the definitional problem of what constitutes architecture, institutional theory is not adept at providing the normative basis necessary for distinguishing between good and bad architecture. The pluralist who adheres to institutional theory may maintain that the merit of a given work is dependent upon the esteem in which the work is held by members of the discipline, but this concept of merit is flawed. Foregoing a highly descriptive phrase about the thing under inquiry in favor of describing a milieu out of which it emerges substitutes one dispassionate phrase for another. The result may be less specificity than we had hoped for, but it is not pernicious. However, substituting the normative content of the same definition—in our case, that "architecture is something that provides both beauty and function" for "architecture is something that architects do"— is to throw out a definition capable of normative content for one that is deliberately stripped of such content. This is an important purpose of institutional theory—to strip definitions of art, or what constitutes an art form, of its troublesome normative content.

What an institutional definition no longer allows the pluralist to do is to rely on a definition of architecture as having anything directly to do with merit or worth. The merit of a piece of architecture now depends on the esteem in which it is held by those in the know. The pluralist's argument and judgment hinges on the legitimacy of this value-bestowing body, rather than on the value of the actual building under consideration. This may be exactly where the pluralist wants the problem to land. He or she may believe that value ultimately rests in human institutions.

But the problem of justification only pauses here, not rests. Before institutional theory was invoked, a work's merit depended upon whether it provided both utility and beauty—that is, whether it crossed the definitional threshold. But to say that a work crosses the institutional threshold—that it meets the criteria for inclusion by those in the know—is not yet to say anything normative about the work itself. Here is where the problem of justification regains momentum; are those in the know motivated by an interest in merit, and if so, are they going to justify merit institutionally as well, or are they going to refer to other criteria? If they are willing to refer to other than institutional criteria, why not skip the institutional step in the first place? If those in the know justify their preferences by referring to the preferences of this same group, then the justification must be coercive, or else it is circular. They may avoid coercion and circularity by justifying the legitimacy of their preferences in relation to the assent of an even larger institution—the nation, the West, or ultimately, the world's present and future population—but this takes the problem of valuing a work of architecture into suspect territory. There is little reason to believe that the population of those in the know is anything but self-elected. They have no mandate of any kind from the population at large. In the absence of such a mandate, the institution that is bestowing merit on given works can only claim to be doing so for itself. Nietzsche would have been pleased by the bold assertion that the good is what serves the ends of the elite, but the rest of us might wish to look elsewhere before resigning ourselves to this. The institutional definition only puts off the problem of assigning merit by a step; the pluralist has not been helped off the horns of his dilemma by this move.

An important distinction needs to be made at this point between pluralistic ideals and plural values as a basis for judgment. The former are motivating in a way that the latter are not. As an ideal, pluralism promotes the expression of diverse viewpoints, something we can all get behind. But as a basis for judgment, it is lacking. We can, for example, easily make sense of the motivating force behind the aesthete's judgment that "despite its functional failings, the Guggenheim is a success because it is so elegant," or the opposing judgment that "despite its beauty, the Guggenheim must be judged a failure because it simply does not work for its intended purpose." We cannot, however, make sense of the logic that "despite its aesthetic success, the Guggenheim's functional shortcomings result in its failure to meet the criteria of a pluralistic outlook, and it is therefore deemed a failure." The latter is not a nonsensical statement, but it assumes something about a belief in the value of pluralism that is foreign to the theory. It assumes that meeting the standard of being plural is one of the goods in the same way as does meeting the standard of being elegant or useful. This is simply not the case. No one will ever rally behind the banner, "Viva Pluralism!" Its best justification is as an instrument to some other good, be it democracy, a vibrant popular culture, respect for others, or the like.

SYNTHESIS

Architectural judgment is supposed to entail a notion of synthesis, a recognition that one is dealing with impure mixtures that must somehow be given order and considered rationally. On the subject of synthesis, any of the three positions examined here could make some claims. The aesthete could reply to the question, "How can you admire the aesthetics of the Guggenheim when it is the aesthetic that makes it unworkable?" by answering that, in fact, his

103

enthusiasm is tempered a bit by this consideration and that he ranks the Guggenheim a notch or two below Wright's Unity Temple, for instance, where the synthesis of form and function is marvelous, precisely for that reason. The aesthete has taken the disvalue of the Guggenheim's poor utility into consideration and finds it aesthetically less pleasing than it would otherwise be. Mary Devereaux calls this outlook "sophisticated formalism" to distinguish it from plain or strict formalism.[10] Sophisticated formalism not only attends to the formal character of the work, but also "tracks the relation" between form and content: Devereaux maintains, "A work's aesthetic achievement consists in the skill with which it expresses its content." Ignoring for the time being the vagueness of the idea of "expressing" content, one can see that with sophisticated formalism, the aesthete has at least a handle on making an inclusive evaluation of a work. Furthermore, he or she achieves this without losing the "distinction between aesthetic and moral evaluation."[11]

One might yet doubt, along with Devereaux, whether the moral point of view has been adequately taken into consideration by this move. If the Guggenheim functions poorly, and if the aesthetic is what causes this, is this not a colossal failure in architectural synthesis? Surely, the answer is "yes." From the point of view of synthesis, it fares badly. The one refuge the sophisticated formalist might claim from this judgment is that his or her praise is not for the building itself, but for the aesthetic ideas it represents. If this is the case, there really is nothing problematic in the aesthete's point of view: He or she can join the moralists and the mainstream in deploring the building's lack of synthesis, while admiring it for other reasons. This might be a tempting argument for the aesthete to take up, but it is unlikely to hold up under scrutiny.

Devereaux thinks that in order to adequately judge works that challenge conventional interpretation we must "broaden the concept of the aesthetic beyond its traditional boundaries," so that we can be said to be judging a work of art aesthetically, "not only when we respond to its formal elements or to the relationship between its formal elements and its content, but also whenever we respond to a feature that makes a work the work of art it is."[12] The question is, does such a remodeling of the concept cast a wide enough net to cover exceptional situations without losing the distinctive outlook we call aesthetic? This seems both doubtful and unnecessary. When faced with an exceptional challenge, one can either "beef up" one's ability to respond, as Devereaux suggests, or call in reinforcements from other disciplines. Rather than develop an all-purpose outlook, why not keep the recognizably aesthetic outlook but be ready to question and bolster it when it no longer seems adequate for the task at hand? Its inadequacy can be regarded as a failure of conventional aesthetic theory, as Devereaux evidently believes, or it can be regarded as an inevitable limitation of an otherwise useful outlook.

The strict moralist seems to have a better claim than the aesthete to having taken the synthetic approach to architectural values into account in his negative assessment. But he would have to be thoroughly perplexed at why so many otherwise intelligent, rational, and well-meaning architects disagree with his judgment. How could he explain this discrepancy? He is not allowed by his outlook to dismiss the matter as a mere dispute over taste. Characterizing the architects who hold these buildings in high esteem as unbalanced, confused, or mean-spirited is not likely to be convincing either.

One might lay claim to the idea that a multileveled evaluation is occurring. On one level are positive aesthetic and negative functional judgments, on a more abstract level, negative synthetic judgment. The synthetic level is informed by, but not more important than, the level of aesthetic and functional judgments. The moralist could then say that those who judge these buildings favorably are paying attention to one level of evaluation, while paying attention to another. There may be some validity to this, in the sense that aesthetic reactions and functional assessments must occur prior to synthetic judgment—otherwise, there would be nothing to synthesize. But it would take further justification before maintaining that judgmental priority means greater specificity and that specific judgments can always be trumped by more abstract ones. In the case of the Guggenheim, this is the question at hand: whether aesthetic success can be so great that use concerns, and hence synthetic concerns, recede in importance. For the strict moralist to say, "of course synthetic judgments always trump judgments on individual values" and that therefore his or her concern for synthesis provides a more adequate judgment, is to beg the question. The aesthete may not be able to lay much claim to having climbed the synthetic pinnacle, but that does not automatically lead to the conclusion that his or her point of view is the inferior one. He or she may, for instance, join Nietzsche in finding the moralist's view to be the flawed one.

An impasse has been reached. The aesthete can only offer a partial evaluation of the Guggenheim. The strict moralist will simply condemn a person's admiration for it. The pluralist must decide between two less-than-ideal alternatives; relativism and an artificial narrowing of what can be considered architecture. Neither aesthetic priority, functional priority, nor something in-between have provided an adequate framework for evaluating conflicts in architectural judgment. Moral theory stands to provide a perspective on the impasse.

The term "strict moralist" has been employed here to identify an outlook that occupies the opposite end of the spectrum from the aesthete. This terminology is also meant to distinguish that point of view from that offered by moral theory. Moral theory may construct views of right and wrong, but it also operates on the meta-level to offer perspectives on the whole business of making moral constructions. These perspectives may champion the moral point of view or they may, instead, insist on its limitations.

Many ways of distinguishing between types of moral theories exist. Distinctions between outcome-oriented and deontological or agent-centered and agent-neutral theories are frequently drawn. For the purposes here, a distinction between those that furnish universal measures and those focused on a more local, tailored approach will be employed.[13]

Universal moralities have their appeal. By developing a principle or set of principles to cover every situation, they promise consistency, rationality, and resonance with conventional ideas about what it means to act from a moral point of view—impartially, fairly, and with the big picture in mind. Universal moralities even question whether an attitude without universal pretensions can be considered a morality at all. Utilitarianism, the doctrine of acting so as to maximize the good, is a universalizing morality, as is the Kantian deontological formulation grounded in the concept of free will. These doctrines are intended to apply to everyone, equally, and at all times.

The utilitarian ideal of maximizing the good judges all actions and all other goods according to the amount of overall utility they contribute to the world. Lacking an ultimate conception of good, utilitarianism would be unable to either

107

maximize or universalize. The problem with defining aesthetic goods as a form of utility are manifold. It is utterly vague, despite many noteworthy attempts to define it, just what sort of utility art is supposed to provide that distinguishes it from other activities. Added to this, valuing art solely for its contribution to the world's utility alienates its supposed value from the motivation to pursue it. Anyone who pursues art—as either creator or patron—for the good it will do in the world has at best only a glancing interest in art.

The problems of vagueness and alienation are but two aspects of the critique of utilitarianism. Another prominent aspect is that maximizing rationality called for by utilitarianism takes inadequate account of the uniqueness of individuals. Utilitarianism demands impartiality. From an impartial point of view, who actually benefits (or suffers) from a decision or course of action is unimportant as long as the benefits are maximized. This outlook fails to recognize that it matters to the person involved whether the good accrues to him or to someone else.[14] One could charge that the tendency to admire the Guggenheim is due in part to the fact that the admirers are not the ones trying to use buildings.

This is not to charge the admirers of the Guggenheim with insensitivity to another person's plight, but to suggest that judging this building impartially may be the wrong orientation from which to judge it. The museum's curators might also admire their building, but for the fact that they are the ones who have to use it. This is not just a matter of asserting that certain people's judgment is better due to their familiarity with the building. The problem that the uniqueness of individuals poses to maximizing calculations is that such calculations have no method for factoring in the difference between you and not me suffering, or me and not you benefiting. This characteristic of maximizing moralities is

108

intentional, because to do otherwise would be opposed to the maintenance of the impartial point of view required by utilitarianism and similar constructions. Utilitarians equate asserting one's individuality with egoism; that is to say, they think that morality depends on one's ability not to assert one's priorities over others.[15]

Thus, utilitarianism's critics might observe that what is wrong with a person's high esteem of the Guggenheim derives from his or her adherence to a point of view that gives insufficient consideration to the disutility this building visits upon those most immediately affected by it as a basis for determining the building's overall merits or failures. By this account, the museum's admirers are sufficiently removed from the building so as to allow the utilitarian outlook to seem natural. But people close to the building come to their judgment from a more personal orientation.

This argument is promising for several reasons. First, it bridges moral and aesthetic domains in a direct, uncomplicated way. Second, it explains how one group could admire this building while another could find it wanting, by taking into consideration an aspect of moral evaluation heretofore missing. What it considers is the idea that who suffers, and how much they suffer, matters. It would be unreasonable to expect those suffering with the use problems created by the Guggenheim's design to regard its aesthetic merit from an impartial outlook. It also assumes that if the building's admirers are unreasonable, then either they are cold and unfeeling people or something is askew in the value system they apply to the building.

This is an interesting line of thought, but it is vulnerable to a utilitarian rejoinder. One wonders if all aesthetic appreciation—often characterized as requiring a certain distance from the object of appreciation—could be called "inappropriately impartial." Admirers of the Guggenheim could rebuff this by arguing that their aesthetic appreciation is very personal to them. They could further assert that the building's detractors are making an implicit benefit calculation of their own, that their own suffering with the building's use problems is more important than the benefits derived from aesthetic appreciation. This rebuff only redirects the argument away from the idea of clashing values onto the utilitarians' impartiality.

Utilitarians should press their case further, by demanding to know how asserting the importance of individuals differs from egoism on the one hand and from asserting (from an impartial outlook) the overall importance of respecting one another on the other. After all, the benefit of mutual respect is something that utilitarians can get behind as easily as their detractors, who assert a more personal orientation.[16]

KANT'S SOLUTION

Kantian morality, with its grounding in rationality and emphasis on the importance of motives in determining the correct action, stands to inform this discussion in new ways. Kant even provides an aesthetic theory, in his *Critique of Judgment*, to mesh with his moral construct. For Kant, the judgment of beauty aspires to universality, just as does the judgment of morality. This places aesthetic judgment on similar footings with moral judgment, "only that [aesthetic judgment] is merely contemplative and does not bring about an interest in the Object; whereas in the moral judgement it is practical."[17] This leads to Kant's famous notion about the disinterestedness of aesthetic judgment: "Beauty is the form of finality in an object, so far as perceived in it apart from the representation of an end."[18] The ambition of morality to universality is through a concept of what makes an action or judgment correct. But, according to Kant, the aesthetic judgment, being much more

110

akin to sense perception, does not entail a concept. "The beautiful pleases immediately,"[19] he writes. Kant goes on to argue that aesthetic ideas "are essentially different from rational ideas of determinate ends."[20] He distinguishes between two kinds of beauty: free beauty, like that of a flower, and ideal beauty, which is attached to some concept of use. Ideal beauty cannot be a pure judgment of taste, but must have an intellectual component. It is attached to an idea of perfection. A work of architecture, it stands to reason, may have judgments of both free and ideal beauty present—free in the sense of aesthetic formalism, and ideal in the sense of how gracefully it achieves its use-ends. Kant could explain the dilemma posed by the Guggenheim as a conflict between two different conceptions of beauty, both of which come to bear in the case of architectural judgment. This conception allows the aesthetic its autonomous place in the world as an instance of free beauty, but allies it with motives and ends that are the province of morality in the case of ideal beauty.

When free and ideal beauty conflict, as they seem to at the Guggenheim, what does the philosopher instruct us to do? Kant believed that aesthetic experience was based in the "harmonious play between imagination and understanding."[21] It is then not a stretch to characterize the problematic nature of the Guggenheim to be that this mental activity reaches a discord when it comes to considering the interplay of form and function. The building fails, not only in terms of utility, but aesthetically as well, because mental discord results when one engages in its aesthetic contemplation. The imagination is inclined to approval, but then understanding steps in with its very rational reservations based on knowledge of the building's functional shortcomings. The result is internal conflict, or disharmony. That Kant should make aesthetic value out to be a form of pleasure after so thoroughly rejecting the role of pleasure in his

111

ethics should come as no surprise; he saved it for just this purpose. In terms set out by a Kantian notion of morality, one could criticize Wright for failing in his duties as an architect to insure that his design met a certain standard of function. This is a legitimate point. But if the recognition that the architect failed in his duty does not translate as well into a lower estimation of the building's worth, the effort will have been pointless, at least for the purpose of bridging aesthetics and morality.

The Guggenheim is sufficiently admired to blunt any assertion that this kind of carry-over has, in fact, occurred. Why bother criticizing the architect for failing in his duty if one is going to go on admiring a building? Such criticism would ring hollow. A Kantian might argue that the building failed in a duty it had, too, but an inanimate object such as a building can be said to have a duty only in a metaphorical sense. One may sensibly dislike a building and the ideas it represents, but one can hardly take a building to task for misbehaving.

Kant's account contains several ideas that serve to recommend it. The internal discord that Kant describes does resemble an aspect of the mental push-and-pull that appreciation of such buildings entails. Furthermore, Kant's analysis makes room for explicit distinctions between aesthetic and moral attitudes. This account does not require us to stretch one or the other conception to accommodate limitations of interpretation. At least one proponent of the Kantian conception, however, thinks that this attitude has further implications as well that many architects would find distasteful.

Anthony Savile argues that Kant's conception of aesthetic experience implies that internal disharmony also results from buildings that are conceived too sculpturally—that is, carved, as it were, out of pure forms, rather than assembled from more or less conventional parts. Savile writes, "To have an architectural character, it must have it through the thought that it is as a building that we are to consider and appreciate it."[22] He uses this argument to single out such modern sculptural buildings as I. M. Pei's addition to the Louvre, Richard Rogers' Lloyds of London building, and Richard Meier's High Museum for disapproval. He approves, instead, of more traditional buildings, which conform to more conventional norms and thus please both the imagination and the understanding.

Where structures such as the Parthenon would fall according to Savile's outlook is dicey. Surely, the Parthenon was conceived as much for its sculptural effect atop the Acropolis as for any other programmatic function. Aesthetic considerations of the Parthenon, then, would create the same mental discord Savile attributes to the work of Pei, Rogers, and Meier. It seems reasonable to expect, however, that any mainstream theory of architecture would make the Parthenon a central, rather than marginal, example of aesthetic achievement. What seems to be at issue in Savile's argument is that he makes the conventional out to be a norm, rather than a constraint on our abilities to think normatively. Savile's take may, of course, simply be wrong, but the fact that this odd argument comes from a Kantian supporter is evidence of a potentially troubling aspect of the theory—that it becomes normative when no such judgment is needed.

Part of the problem with the Guggenheim is not that it causes so much inner conflict within people's "faculties of cognition,"[23] but that people—and architects in particular— feel so much unreserved affection for it. The problem is not so much, "How do I cope with all this inner discord?" but "How do I reconcile my admiration of these buildings with the fact of obvious failings which I normally regard to be important?" or put another way, "Why don't I feel more inner discord than I do?" Like the sophisticated formalist, the Kantian prefers that the building's failings inform one's aesthetic judgment by

113

creating inner disharmony and that this disharmony be reflected in a lower estimation for these works. But this does not work for Kant any better than it does for the sophisticated formalist. This move fails because it tries to substitute one kind of value—the inner harmony in the play of the faculties of cognition—for a different kind of value—the aesthetic value of the building itself. This is not a case of subjective versus objective value; it is as possible to be objective in one's analysis of mental processes as it is about buildings. Rather, this is a case of making one's admiration and affection for architecture out to be merely instrumental for the achievement of some other good; for Kant, this good is a form of pleasure.

One reason it makes sense to consider Kant's moral and aesthetic conceptions to be all of a piece is his assertion that we understand aesthetic worth to be symbolic of the morally good. By "symbolic," Kant means "an indirect presentation of the concept by means of an analogy." The analogy of the moral presented by things we find beautiful has two functions: first, it makes a mental concept concrete in a way that the senses can apprehend, and second, it provides a kind of conduit for reflecting on the moral concept itself.[24] But this analogy is problematic with regard to the example here, because the Guggenheim's aesthetic merit seems to serve as much to overshadow its failings of use as to illuminate its moral worth. The Kantian would be in a dilemma here—for either the analogy created by beauty is sometimes misleading, in which case Kant's assertion about the symbolic nature of beauty had best be arrested, or else the Kantian would need to assert that we are just trying to draw the wrong lessons out of the beauty of this building. We should be drawing other, less obvious, analogies.

Kant's attempts to carve out distinctive areas of influence for the aesthetic and the moral seem promising, but some of the implications that have been drawn, rightly or wrongly, from this observation raise more questions than this discussion can properly address. The Kantian starts off with some simple, elegant distinctions between the aesthetic and the moral: that aesthetic experience involves a form of pleasure but that morality excludes justification in pleasure, and that morality must be deeply imbedded in rationality, while the aesthetic is rooted in the imagination. Using these distinctions, however, to help pin down the relationship between the aesthetic and the ethical has proven unsuccessful.

COMMON SUBJECT MATTER

Kant is not alone in noting a metaphorical intimacy between aesthetic and moral ideas. E. H. Gombrich speaks of "noble simplicity" and artistic "negation, restraint, or renunciation" and of how these ideas might carry connotations into both the aesthetic and the moral spheres.[25] Gombrich goes on, however, to warn against the "temptation to take the metaphor literally," maintaining that art's metaphorical bridging to the moral is not a reliable indicator of moral virtue or goodness.[26] Here, a potentially important point can be made: While aesthetic judgments such as that a work exhibits "noble simplicity" cannot be taken to literally constitute a moral judgment of the work itself, one can—as Gombrich does— take notice of the fact that the characteristics a culture values in a work of art are indicative of what culture values in a larger, moral sense. Issues of aesthetic value become a microcosm for a culture's overall values. Gombrich notes, for instance, that in our time the "static social values of 'noble' versus 'vulgar' are replaced by the 'dynamic' values of 'progressive' versus 'backward.'"[27] In this way, a certain cross-fertilization between the moral and aesthetic can be postulated. The judgment of aesthetic goodness is not a reliable measuring stick of moral goodness, but the subject matter of what constitutes aesthetic worth both influences and is reflective of social value in the largest sense. The moralist and the artist (or critic) are frequently concerned with the same kinds of problems. Think of how Walter Gropius and Le Corbusier embraced the challenge to architectural creativity posed by mechanization. Aesthetic judgment becomes fodder for moral consideration when it challenges conventional interpretation.

How might Gombrich's observation that art and morality often address the same cultural issues play out in this discussion? In the Guggenheim, Wright addressed the circulation "problem" of maze-like galleries where one is constantly doubling back through rooms already visited. The architect took on a distinct "problem" posed by modern life; a problem posed both to function and aesthetics.

The moralist might speculate that in this case, the solution to the "problem" was so poorly executed in functional terms that the architect could not have been very interested in anything but esthetic problems and that these functional issues were more like pretexts than objectives. The architect effectively seized on this commission as an excuse to explore certain artistic interests, regardless of whether the forms he employed were appropriate. On the other hand, the concept of "appropriate" is highly normative in itself. Some architects' decisions are bound to be arbitrary, in the sense of not being completely determined by the problem. To make a stronger statement, it could be said that Wright went beyond the pale in this building and exhibited an arrogance, abuse of trust, or blatant disregard for important human needs. The moralist would then at least have an argument. This conclusion, however, seems unnecessarily harsh.

The aesthete would certainly be more forgiving on this point, even if he or she granted that Wright's aesthetic agenda conflicted with his functional one. He or she might argue that the discrepancy between this building's aesthetic success and poor functional showing was not due to an abuse of power, but was an outgrowth of a fundamental conflict of interests. This conclusion goes too easily on the architect, however. In the case of professional practice, the architect enters into ready-made circumstances invariably in need of mediation. In an individual building design, it would be abdicating too much responsibility to say that the mediation of aesthetics and function necessarily contains built-in conflicts. The architect's actions often determine whether aesthetics and function will seriously conflict. Examples of modernist functionalism from the early twentieth century and of the high-tech movement in the 1970s serve to demonstrate that architects can successfully embrace function as the source of their aesthetic. This would argue against the idea that the gap between aesthetics and function is insurmountable.

Gombrich's observation that aesthetics and morality often share the same subject matter is promising, but it plays out poorly against the moralist's and aesthete's points of view in the case of the Guggenheim. If Wright truly did not care about the functional shortcomings of his building, he would have taken its functional considerations even less seriously than he did. One would expect this heartless disregard for people's needs to catch up with the architect in more thoroughgoing ways than it has. The moralist is eventually brought to attack Wright's devotion to service, rather than face the prospect of a gap between aesthetic and moral merit to explain his building's poor functional showing. Making the problem of judging aesthetic and use values together to be a matter of the architect's character is a poor solution, but the aesthete has no satisfying way to explain the disjunction between aesthetic and functional success under Gombrich's model either. The idea that a reconciliation between aesthetics and function can be forged on the basis of common subject matter seems to have reached a dead end for the universalist.

An important critique of moral theories such as utilitarianism and Kantian deontic theory is that they so overrate the importance of consistency in moral judgments that they reduce the otherwise conceptually rich content of morality to one concept of the good.[28] In the case of consequentialist theories like utilitarianism, this one concept is to maximize the good in the world. For Kant, the ultimate measure was acting from the motive of duty. This has its parallel in architecture, where in the twentieth century the discipline has struggled to be concerned with essential, universal problems, and has dismissed the local or conventional as being less important. The attachment to universal, reductionistic morality leads to what has been called a "thin" conception of morality or of moral good.

"Thin" moral concepts tend to "thin out" ethical thinking in two ways. First, they isolate the evaluative component of moral thinking from the factual by employing words like "good," "bad," "right," "wrong," "ought"—words that express a broad, universal evaluation. This is in contrast to such words that convey concepts such as "cowardly," "generous," "brutal," "false," "pompous," "snobbish," "humble." These concepts "seem to express a union of fact and value."[29] The second way in which thin concepts thin out ethical thinking is to try and reduce it to one ultimate concept, whether it be human happiness, eudaemonia, good will, or some other ultimate good.

'Thick' concepts, on the other hand, do not depend upon claims of universality. In any given situation, a number of thick

118

concepts might apply. They are not mutually exclusive in the way that good and bad are, nor are they redundant in the way that are good and right. Thick concepts are also open to unseating by reflection, but to the extent that they survive close examination, they are more stable than thin concepts. The judgments made by employing thick concepts can be straightforwardly true, and the claim involved in assenting to them can be correspondingly honored.[30]

This distinction between two types of ethical thinking has a close parallel in how architecture is typically judged in the architectural press. Thomas Fisher described what may be called "thin" architectural judgment when he wrote,

> The problem lies in the disconnect between reportage and evaluation, the latter being only loosely linked to the project's requirements and challenges and to the architect's intentions and restrictions . . . . [The result is that] the typical feature article in an architectural magazine reveals this confusion between fact and feeling. Most articles begin with an opening to draw the reader in, then describe the project and its development, and conclude with the author rendering an opinion."[31]

As a result, the critic is more likely to feel comfortable judging a work of architecture to be "significant" or "derivative" rather than "gregarious," say, or "standoffish." It is not hard to sense the relative thinness of the former in relation to the latter.

Keeping architectural evaluation thin achieves several things for the writer; it allows the discussion to proceed on a more objective plane until it is time for a summation. It allows the writer to avoid stating and defending a distinct point of view. It is less likely to antagonize the architects whose work is under discussion than would an unapologetically partisan, opinionated discussion. The problem with thin evaluation

119

from the standpoint of the judgments needed here lies in the disconnect Fisher describes between reportage and evaluation and in the inability to entertain multiple interpretations. A thin discussion presumes the availability of a summary judgment based on universal principles—that is, a privileged position from outside the interpretation of the work from which to deliver an overall judgment. One must, in principle, be able to express a generally favorable or unfavorable review after all is said. If one traded in this presumption for the concept that all one can hope to provide is an interpretation from a necessarily limited perspective—one that makes no claim to an objective standpoint—the summary judgment, if indeed there is one at all, would be implied by the discussion, rather than necessarily stated. But a presumption of the ability to sum up a building's worth may not be needed at all. If, for example, one were to discuss Wright's museum, as Mumford suggests, in terms of its being mechanical, coercive, single-minded, and deterministic, the discussion that would naturally follow in its wake would center on the resonance and intelligence of such an interpretation, rather than on its objectivity. A thick discussion allows the reader to do more than merely stack up reasons to agree or disagree with the critic's final judgment; it allows the reader to get inside the interpretation itself and play with the point of view being offered up. The degree to which the interpretation withstands such pulling and stretching is an indication of its worth.

Users of thick concepts, then, have traded in a claim to truth or to ultimate value for durability—for ideas and expressions of value that are subject to objections and disagreements of all kinds, but which withstand such assaults with their meanings more or less intact. Unlike thin concepts, they do not ultimately rest on claims of transcendence. Rather, they derive their legitimacy from within conventions of beliefs and desires that constitute our resource for ordinary everyday rationality. While thick concepts may reflect a systematic unity of aim, they—unlike utilitarianism and similar theories—do not depend on such a unity for legitimacy. The claim of durability in this regard demands less commitment to any particular moral theory than do concepts of ultimate or foundational correctness, in that thick concepts need claim nothing special about themselves beyond limited applicability to the task at hand. This is in contrast to, say, the ultimate utilitarian good of human happiness, which, as the final good, must go untested: nothing exists of greater scope against which to measure it. That evaluative words such as "generosity" and "parsimonious" invite reflection upon their applicability to a given situation, whereas words like "right" and "wrong" invite a more removed consideration, also counts in favor of thicker expressions. Not only is the immediacy of thick words a benefit, but these concepts lean toward richer, and thus more satisfying, language for the expression and evaluation of aesthetic motives.

Elizabeth Anderson identifies three features of thick concepts:

> Their applications are determined by interpretive processes that employ evaluative reasoning
>
> Their coherence depends on the social practices and contexts that make their proper attitudes intelligible.
>
> They tend to evolve in reciprocal interaction with their proper attitudes.[32]

An obvious structural similarity between thick moral concepts and aesthetic concepts arises: "Aesthetic evaluative concepts, such as of the beautiful, the goofy, and the quaint, guide such responses as admiring contemplation, disparaging amusement, and nostalgia."[33] Thick aesthetic and thick ethical concepts tend to use the same words. Such concepts as graceful and awkward, playful and dour, engaging and aloof, accessible and haughty, inviting and self-involved, courageous and craven, or bold and anonymous, have both moral and aesthetic meanings, and they encourage a person to think about architecture in a richer vocabulary than do more analytic terms, which isolate the aesthetic facts from evaluations of those facts. Analytic terms such as heavy, light, geometric, rectilinear, textured, smooth, layered, monumental, exuberant, and those perennial favorites of the glossy magazines, crisp and taut, which stick to non-evaluative facts about things, discourage contrast with their potentially interesting evaluative counterparts: bloated, waifish, idealistic, soft, hard, accessible, overbearing, hysterical, and the improbable opposites, soggy detailing and flabby volumes. Separating the descriptive from the evaluative allows the critic to appear more scientific, dispassionately gathering a preponderance of data before taking a stand on the aesthetic merits of a building. The cost of this approach is that the breadth of the discussion is restricted.

For example, rather than discuss the Guggenheim in the instrumental terms of problems in artistic consumption and display, we might instead keep the discussion closer to and more focused on the building and the art. We could note, disapprovingly, that the whale-sized atrium tends to swallow the art, that the squinchy, cave-like viewing spaces are cruel to paintings, and that the building is haughtily indifferent to these problems. We could also speak approvingly of the building's beckoning, audacious playfulness against the otherwise dour section of Fifth Avenue and of its nose-thumbing adolescent exuberance against the "tasteful" palatial-style art gallery. And can we not make a serious case for asserting that it is the possibility of these sorts of reactions, rather than utilitarian ones, that makes architecture the source of fascination that it is? Thin conceptions, with their insistence on objectivity, ironically and stubbornly refuse to let humans forget themselves. These thick conceptions tend toward the fanciful, yes, but they also allow us to engage the world more directly, more vividly.

By attaching the moral sphere of architecture to a limited conception, rather than to a universal system, a person may regard both aesthetics and utility from a new point of view— one that is recognizably moral, although not necessarily consistent in its judgments. How this applies to the problem of judging the virtues and shortcomings of the Guggenheim and other problematic buildings is not at all obvious. Even though thick ethical concepts share a common language with thick aesthetic concepts, it does not follow that the terms mean the same thing within the contexts of their usage. Arnold Isenberg, for instance, argues that "pretentious art, though it cannot be too severely criticized on aesthetic grounds, probably does not deserve any moral rebuke. An aesthetic pretension need not entail or reveal any other pretension whatsoever."[34] What does follow, however, is that using the same language allows us to align the two discussions much more closely than has been heretofore possible. This development is a good thing.

Does this leave the problem of judging the likes of the Guggenheim where it began, with the rather unhelpful conclusion that it is artistically distinguished but a poor functional performer? Or has the discussion gathered some concepts with which judging the aesthetic successes of these works can be informed by knowledge of their functional shortcomings, and vice versa? Such buildings pose a problem to architectural judgment because they defy conventional frameworks for interpretation. Neither the aesthete's, the moralist's, nor the pluralist's point of view is sufficient by itself to make the desired connections, and these outlooks appear to preclude each other. Universalist moral theories, such as

123

those provided by utilitarianism and by Kantian deontological thinking, provide perspective on the problem, but the utilitarian's insistence on impartiality makes it hard to understand why these works pose a judgment problem in the first place, and Kant's theory of the analogy between the aesthetically pleasing and the good provides neither a strong nor reliable connection between aesthetic worth and moral value. Modernists and their offspring make the kind of judgments sought here more difficult to endorse by their tacit acceptance of the authority of the utilitarian outlook. A more conceptually rich outlook—one that stands to aid in forming the kinds of judgments desired—is possible by means of employing thick evaluative concepts. But even though this idea closely aligns ethical and aesthetic vocabularies, it does not follow that a synthetic judgment is necessarily possible. Thus, the desired connection between the moral and the aesthetic, although strengthened, is still relatively weak.

We are left without a definitive solution to the problem of judging such convention-shattering buildings as the Guggenheim, but with a better understanding of the difficulties this and others buildings like it present to aesthetic and moral judgment due to their grounding in convention. Not all buildings pose such problems, but architects in particular are often attracted to works that "break all the rules." Architectural history is studded with examples of well-regarded architects who ignored conventional constraints and created memorable buildings. The Crystal Palace, the Eiffel Tower, the Robie House, the Sydney Opera House, the Pompidou Center, and the Bilbao Guggenheim are but a few examples. Some structures were immediate successes; with others, it took some time before the challenges they posed to interpretation were met. The deep difficulties to judgment posed by the Guggenheim may serve as a cautionary tale to designers.

124

Unlike his Robie House, which resides comfortably within the pantheon of great twentieth-century architecture, Wright's Guggenheim occupies a sort of architectural purgatory. Although the esteem with which it is held among architects has increased with time, final judgment may never be passed, because as yet no means exist to make such a judgment. This makes such buildings interesting cases to discuss, but perhaps not to emulate.

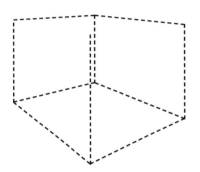

CHAPTER 5 | FIRMITAS

The interpretation of building codes has been the subject of a recurring debate within architectural and engineering circles for many years. This debate revolves around the central question of whether building codes and similar regulations should be regarded as providing a target level of public amenity, a minimum level, or a maximum level. Practice usually dictates that the code be regarded as a target, to be exceeded as little as possible. Only occasionally do designers regard the regulations as providing a maximum, with one notable exception being the commonplace request for variances from stringent zoning laws. Designers rarely regard the code as providing a minimum. This would require designers to justify to their clients why they are committing to more than the law requires—this, despite the fact that the codes themselves are invariably written as minimum performance standards.[1] By regarding code requirements as targets or as maximums, architects and engineers are, in effect, regarding building codes in a way that they were not meant to be interpreted.

Some designers would object to this statement. They believe that the codes are written with generous factors of safety included in structural calculations, units of egress, and the like. Following the code as a target is perfectly acceptable, because the writers of the code know full well how they will be regarded in practice. The recent history of building codes, and to a lesser extent, zoning regulations, would tend to confirm this belief. Codes are increasingly being written as performance standards, thus placing greater emphasis on the designer's knowledge and methods, and less on codes as prescriptions that must be followed to the letter.[2]

This evolution in the nature of building codes reinforces the idea that professional moral obligations exist within a network of well-defined relationships, expectations, and activities. If the fit between what the design professional provides and what is expected of him or her by clients and by society is a good one, then the professional's moral obligations are not problematic. Because clients and the public have a fairly clear idea of what they are receiving from their design professionals in terms of structural performance, fire safety, and other aspects related to the *firmitas* of a building—clear because these performance standards are frequently tested and amended in real life situations—it matters little whether a discrepancy exists between the stated intention of a building code and how it is actually regarded in practice. This is why the debate over building codes has remained merely a matter of interest, rather than urgency.

If this well-understood net of obligations is transgressed, however, the moral aspects of construction suddenly become problematic. An enormous amount of public trust, to say nothing of life safety, is riding both on the designer meeting society's needs and on society using its buildings as they were meant to be used. Building owners cannot, for instance, use residential structures as theaters, parking garages as libraries, or store hazardous chemicals in public bathrooms; nor can an architect construct stairwells out of combustible materials, fail to include tie-downs in high-wind areas, or ignore snow loads in cold climates.

But transgressions, either deliberate or arising from neglect, are not the only way in which the moral dimension enters one's thinking about the durability and structural performance of architecture. If performance standards are based on incomplete empirical evidence, are poorly understood by the public, or frequently change, the ethical aspects of design become problematic as well. In these situations, even the most well-meaning designer can no longer be sure that a building meets public needs and expectations. In these situations, the designer is not only concerned with the relatively straightforward ethical concern of not transgressing his or her obligations, but is also faced with the more vexing problem of establishing just what constitutes these obligations. When this occurs, the designer has left behind the guidance provided by convention and empirical knowledge and, however unwillingly, must seek guidance elsewhere. The obvious place to look for such guidance is his or her ethics.

Although a design professional can and should continue to look toward convention and empirical data to inform his or her decisions, this information may not present itself in a timely manner. One could refuse to engage decisions that require ethical deliberation and abandon the problem to someone else, demand that a political solution be found through a vote or referendum, or even ask for divine guidance. But rather than abandon the decision-making responsibility altogether or turn it over to another party, the design professional can also look to an immediate source of direction: an ethic of practice.

One situation currently faced by design professionals and their clients that engenders such dilemmas is the need to design buildings to withstand the forces generated by earthquakes. The seismic code is based on severely incomplete empirical evidence, is widely misunderstood by the public, and frequently changes. Vitruvius' third source of value, so often relegated to the background in the conflicts between utility and aesthetics, takes front stage in this situation as a matter for ethical deliberation.

PROBLEMS OF INTERPRETING THE SEISMIC CODE

The purpose of a seismic code, like any building code, is to protect life, health, and the public welfare. In ethical terms, such a code regulates certain actions on the basis of their consequences for the public. The mission of the code is quite clear. Since both public and professional sentiment has determined that the opportunity costs of constructing buildings capable of withstanding all conceivable earthquakes without damage are simply too great, the seismic codes have been designed to establish only thresholds of safety. The philosophy of structural seismic safety was first articulated in 1967 in the commentary to the Structural Engineers Association of California (SEAC) *Blue Book*. The target level of safety established by the code specified that structures should resist minor quakes without damage, moderate earthquakes without structural damage, and major earthquakes without collapse. Although the seismic code has changed considerably since then, this statement of mission has not. Seismic codes are written to provide minimum standards for the achievement of this performance level.

A disturbing aspect of the seismic code as it reads today is that the consensus on how to design buildings to perform adequately has changed substantially over time. With code provisions other than seismic, change is slow; little disagreement exists about gravity loads, for instance, and these provisions have withstood untold tests in everyday circumstances. With the seismic code, however, the situation is different. What was considered seismically safe in the 1940s is considered inadequate by current standards. The rapid pace of code change and recent and planned code amendments give us little reason to think that the seismic provisions have reached a period of maturity characteristic of other code sections. (See Chart A.)

Do the codes as written achieve their stated purpose? This question can be answered by empirical investigation. Indeed, much of the work in contemporary seismic research seeks to insure that the code does achieve its purpose. If the answer is yes, then the architects and engineers can proceed unimpeded by ethical issues; should the answer be no, the design professional is faced with a large ethical dilemma. Does the designer accept a code provision that he or she thinks provides less than desirable performance, or craft a personal position regarding the code? Each alternative has its pitfalls.

Assuming, however, that the code is unlikely to be found totally inadequate, a more probable answer to the question of whether it achieves the target level of performance is "yes, with a few reservations." In this case, the dilemma has been lessened, but not eliminated. The design professional will want to isolate the provisions that do not achieve the performance targets. He or she is then faced with a range of possible actions:

Avoid any problem by never relying on these provisions.

Use them anyway.

Use them only when necessary and then only with a higher-than-ordinary level of analysis and care in detailing.

The first and second strategies avoid an ethical dilemma by refusing to engage it directly. These alternatives, however, may only postpone the dilemma or change its terms. The final course of action obliges the professional to overcome at least two further dilemmas, which contain both ethical and technical dimensions, before proceeding. The design professional will

1906	San Francisco earthquake; code established; wind load resistance of 30psf is assumed to account for seismic forces.
1907	Charles Derleth, a founder of the Structural Association (later SEAOC), publishes suggested changes to the code for seismic safety.
1925	Santa Barbara earthquake; US Coast and Geodetic survey begins strong motion studies.
1928	California State Chamber of Commerce sponsors a work authored by the state's leading structural engineers "dedicated to the safe-guarding of buildings against earthquake disaster"; report forms foundation for later codes.
1933	Long Beach earthquake; first strong motion ground shaking records obtained.
1927	UBC provision: $V = CW$.
1933	Los Angeles code: $V = CW$; Field Act covering school construction requires buildings to resist 10% of their vertical dead load + live load laterally; Riley Act covering most other buildings requires buildings to resist 2% of total vertical design load.
1934	Board of Fire Underwriters issues "Recommendations for Earthquake Resistant Design of Buildings, Structure and Tanks"; recommends formula $F = CW$, where the coefficient $C = .10$ for structures, .20 for bearing walls, 1.0 for parapets, cantilevers, and ornament, and .20 for chimneys; W = dead load + 25% of live load.
1939	Garrison Act provides local school boards with power to close unsafe schools.
1943	City of Los Angeles code introduces dynamic properties (based on height); later adopted by UBC.
1953	UBC coefficients changed from a % to a formula $60/(N + 4.5)$, where N is the number of stories above the story under considera-tion; Field Act amended to adopt new design criteria.
1957	San Francisco–Daly City earthquake.
1959	First SEAOC Blue Book (Recommended Lateral Force Requirements and Commentary): $V = KCW$.
1964	Alaska earthquake; anchorage of exterior elements placed in code.
1966	SEAOC presents ductility requirements for reinforced concrete.
1967	First time a philosophy of the code appears (in SEAOC Blue Book commentary); has not changed since.
1967–68	Greene Act requires abandonment of unsafe school buildings by 1975.
1970–73	UBC provisions: $V = ZKCW$.

1971	San Fernando earthquake; first ductility requirements for reinforced concrete appear in ACI code; concept of an importance factor appears after hospitals are severely damaged.
1973–85	Provisions: $V = ZIKCSW$.
1974	Third Blue Book: $V = ZIKCSW$.
1975	California Seismic Safety Commission created by California legislature.
1978	ATC-3-06 (Tentative Provisions for the Development of Seismic Regulations for buildings) released for adoption by all model code agencies; the Applied Technology Council (ATC) works for the National Bureau of Standards and the National Science Foundation; Building Seismic Safety Council undertakes trial designs; ATC-3-06 becomes basis for NEHRP recommended provisions: $V = CsW$.
1979	Establishment of the BSSC to facilitate implementation of the new code provisions; first California State Historical Building Code regulations issued (law passed in 1975).
1983	Coalinga earthquake.
1985	BSSC adopts NEHRP's recommended provisions for the Development of Seismic Regulations for Buildings and promotes it to model code organizations (SBCC, BOCA, CABO, UBC).
1985	Edition of the UBC based on 1974 Blue Book.
1986	New edition of the Blue Book proposes $V = ZICW/Rw$.
1987	Whittier Narrows earthquake.
1988	UBC adopts 1986 SEAOC provisions.
1989	Loma Prieta earthquake; California Essential Services Buildings law effective July 1; Seismic Structural Safety for Hospitals on November 15.
1991	BOCA and SBCC adopt NEHRP provisions; design across the country is based on a 0.2% probability of experiencing an earthquake in any given year which exceeds the resistance of the structure.
1992	Building Standards Commission approves California Code for Building Conservation, effective 7/1/93.

135

have to decide when it is "necessary" to rely on the code and how great an increase in care is required. These are not routine matters. They require reflection and judgment, which can bog down the design process and create additional expense for the design professional. A further investment in empirical investigation is also required to determine the sensible limits of the technologies in question.

Are the performance goals incorporated in the building code satisfactory to begin with? This moral question is informed partly by technical data and partly by professional and personal values. The possible range of opinions spans from complete acceptance of the code as optimizing the difficult trade-offs of cost and safety to its rejection as a wholly inadequate standard for building well. Here, an ethical theory would be most helpful to structure a concept of satisfactory performance. How one prioritizes the competing claims of economy, utility, aesthetics, and safety present in almost any building program influences the answer to this question. Furthermore, how the professional engineer or architect envisions his or her role in society comes to bear on this issue. To make an informed code interpretation, the designer must understand why the concept of adequate construction has changed over time, what considerations remain outside the designer's purview, and what the public needs and expects. The sum of these considerations forms the basis for ethical consideration of the seismic code.

THE PILOT STUDY

If the code does model target levels of performance, and these performance levels are deemed adequate by engineers, researchers, and the public, then little reason would exist to single out the seismic sections of the code for ethical scrutiny.

Little research, however, has gone into determining how the seismic code is, in fact, regarded either by professionals or by the public. In 1992, Peter May and Nancy Stark published the results of a survey of engineers in the Pacific Northwest and found that these professionals largely acquiesced to the code. The firm reported, "At most structural engineers reported seismic codes being substantially exceeded for 15–20% of the structures they design"[3]—this, despite their knowledge that the code presumes that practice will exceed policy. The three most frequently given reasons for why design seldom exceeded code minimum were as follows:

> Designers are comfortable with the existing regulations. The minimum standard is viewed as providing some margin of comfort.
>
> Client budgets—to exceed code requires extra justification.
>
> Cost competitiveness of services—"A client doesn't want a fortress, just a building which functions safely."[4]

What people think in the more seismically active areas of California has gone largely unexplored. To come to some determination on this matter, the cooperation of the Structural Engineers Association of Northern California (SEAONC) was enlisted. A survey was sent to its members that investigated how they regard the seismic provisions of the code. The purpose of the survey was to see if the responses May and Stark received in their survey of the Pacific Northwest would be replicated in a more seismically active area, to test the idea that the changing nature of the seismic code introduced a recognizable set of dilemmas for the engineer, to determine whether a discrepancy existed between how the code was intended to be interpreted and how engineers actually viewed it, and finally, to discern whether the structural design

137

profession's attitudes were in accord with the general public's regarding issues of seismic safety.[5]

The results of the survey indicate that an overwhelming majority of engineers endorsed the philosophy outlined in the *Blue Book*, which maintains that structures should resist minor quakes without damage, moderate earthquakes without structural damage, and major earthquakes without collapse. Much less agreement was found, however, on the question of whether the current provisions of the Uniform Building Code (UBC) actually meet this standard, with just over half agreeing that they did. This perception seems at odds with the widely held view that the vast majority of post-1971 buildings perform much better than the code philosophy reflects, since most modern buildings actually appear to resist major earthquakes with only minor damage. Furthermore, almost everyone agreed that the provisions needed to change to reflect empirical knowledge gained from recent quakes. These results suggest that the large majority of practicing engineers design buildings that perform much better than the code requires, yet are not doing so as a matter of methodology. Perhaps such traditional safeguards as redundancy and factors of safety are to be credited for the performance premium. Such a disparity, even a beneficial one, calls into question just how well structural designers can actually predict the performance of structures. This question becomes ever more urgent as the profession moves into more performance-based specifications.

Most engineers recognize the need to go beyond the code and make personal interpretations as occasions require. This recognition affects practice in several ways. Most respondents report designing buildings to withstand higher lateral forces than required by the UBC at times, and just as many report using detailing standards that they believe to be in excess of

UBC minimums. The use of detailing to improve building performance beyond the minimum is more than just good professional practice. It is also the means by which many engineers attempt to add ductility to a structure—by designing to higher forces without facing potential challenges from building owners and their representatives. Whether these detailing practices actually result in safer buildings is an untested proposition. A majority of engineers also reported avoiding one or two code-permitted structural systems. These systems run the gamut from gypsum board shear walls to concrete moment frames.

Upon "taking matters into their own hands," engineers must decide whether and how to notify others of their actions. One-third of those responding to the survey felt they had the right to require that a building be designed beyond the code minimums without the owner's overt consent and reported having exercised that right on occasion. This illustrates one of the most basic dilemmas of the profession. Honesty is a highly prized commodity among professionals and cannot be violated lightly, but neither can life-safety and the physical well-being of a building's occupants. In cases where, in the engineer's opinion, failing to make a building perform significantly better than the code requires would create questionable, marginal, or unacceptable performance, the engineer is faced with a troubling inner conflict. In these situations, either the client's desires or the public's trust will be confronted.

When facing this dilemma, several possible courses of action present themselves. The structural design professional can,

> Seek another outside opinion, which could either reinforce or vitiate the professional's initial opinion.

> Abdicate the problem to the client, the building authority, or to a strict code interpretation.

> Proceed openly and in accord with one's initial professional opinion, thus inviting dissension and conflict.

> Proceed quietly to implement one's professional opinion, thus likely avoiding conflict with other parties involved in the building process.

Each of these options has its liabilities. While the first alternative is at least initially the most palatable, it is also the one most likely to drag out the problem. If a second opinion confirms the initial one, is this enough to counter any possible objections of the owner, or is a third or fourth opinion sought until the matter is decided by a vote? This alternative also begs the question of whether any other party is likely to know more or have a more qualified opinion than the project designer. Why not simply proceed openly and aggressively in the manner described by the third option? As the responses to the SEAONC survey indicate, this is often easier said than done. An overwhelming majority indicated that option two was unacceptable. Most engineers, at least occasionally, design to withstand greater seismic forces than the code minimums specified. However, many report implementing the fourth option to varying degrees. Such "quiet" strategies included anything from using superior detailing standards to simply plugging larger forces into their calculations.

This study also suggested that regarding the upgrade of existing buildings, the thinking of the structural design profession is in disarray. Approximately two-thirds of those responding to the survey agreed that existing buildings should be retrofitted to lower standards than new buildings. The same percentage reported having designed voluntary seismic upgrades to lower performance levels. Virtually no one, however, reported having stated the performance level in their construction documents. While the idea that some upgrading is better than none is perhaps understandable, the question arises as to whether such upgrades provide a false sense of security to building users and to subsequent owners not a party to the upgrade process. While many Californians are experienced enough to recognize the telltale signs of retrofitting for seismic strength, how many can look at a strengthened building and make some determination about the level of performance to which it was designed? The engineering firm Rutherford & Chekene's 1990 report to the City of San Francisco echoes this concern when it states,

> Despite attempts at educating the general public and building owners concerning realistic performance goals for strengthened buildings, there is a common perception that such a building has been "protected" and that large monetary losses from damage or building downtime no longer need be considered. This is seldom the case with retrofit buildings, particularly [unreinforced masonry buildings].[6]

Even an experienced professional would be hard-pressed to determine something beyond a "yes it was" or "no it wasn't" conclusion.

The results May and Stark obtained in their survey of engineers in the Pacific Northwest engineers did not correspond to those obtained from California engineers. Structural design professionals in California are in widespread agreement with the philosophy of the seismic code, and little internal conflict is evident in areas where the code is well-established. In less codified areas, such as in seismic retrofit, the degree of agreement breaks down. In contrast to their Pacific Northwest colleagues, rather than abdicating the right to widely interpret code provisions, engineers in California recognize and deal with their concerns responsibly and creatively. The problem of retrofitting existing buildings has, however, met with little professional consensus regarding the

141

best way to proceed. This is bad news for the engineering profession, which, like all professions, must depend on a widely shared body of practices and beliefs to exist as such.

Regarding an accord with the public, engineers' overwhelming approval of the current code philosophy is almost certainly at odds with consumer expectations. To test this hypothesis, a group of twenty Rotarians from San Francisco was given a similar, although less comprehensive, survey. These business people made for a reasonably good sample of well-educated, well-informed consumers, many of whom were likely to be involved in decisions involving their places of business. The Rotarians indicated they expect that up-to-date buildings would experience only minor damage when exposed to severe earthquake forces. Although no formal poll of building owners has been taken, the conclusions indicated in Sharpe's informal polling of owners, engineers, and regulatory officials after the Loma Prieta earthquake concur with these results; owners expect something better than merely a salvageable structure.[7]

These findings suggest a significant disparity between the expectations of the public and those of the engineer. This disparity has a negative impact on the value of the pact design professionals have with the public through its agent, the licensing board. As long as modern buildings tend to perform better than the code philosophy specifies, this disparity should pose no undue problems for designers. The over-performance characteristic of modern buildings has likely contributed to this presumption by consumers that buildings will withstand severe earthquakes well. That this over-performance was not always by design is potentially troubling for a profession moving towards a more specific, performance-based methodology—a move which is otherwise welcome as a means of eliminating the gap between public and professional views.

142

The validity of target levels of performance becomes more problematic in the absence of a consensus between design professionals and the public. From the time of the 1933 Long Beach earthquake—the event that initiated the first seismic code in the United States—the public's participation in the code development process has been implied, rather than overt. No town hall meetings are held to demand improved seismic safety; no letter-writing campaigns are directed at the governor; no great clashes occur between those who have foolishly built on seismically dangerous sites and those who have not. The California Seismic Safety Commission must go begging for political support for legislation mandating the upgrade of the state's seismically vulnerable structures.[8] Despite sophisticated public involvement in environmental and social issues, seismic issues are often regarded as too complex for the public's comprehension. Seismic considerations typically take a back seat to concerns over increased infrastructure costs, water allocation issues, and pressures on the public school system in planning new developments. Perhaps people want to ignore the problem, or perhaps they genuinely do not perceive earthquakes as a threat.

Code changes have occurred as a result of the activities of well-meaning professionals and government employees, working (often as volunteers) in what they see as the best interest of the public and therefore in their professional capacity. Organizations such as the SEAOC's seismology committee, the Seismic Safety Commission, the American Technology Council, and the International Conference of Building Officials are committed to improving the knowledge and building methodologies surrounding seismic design so that

143

responsible decisions can be made. The Seismic Safety
Commission expresses this dilemma when it states,

> An overriding question that arises from the Commission's
> study of the effects of the Northridge earthquake on
> buildings is "What level of risk to the public is
> acceptable?" . . . We could build nothing but square one-
> story houses with few windows on flat ground well away
> from any known fault; that would minimize earthquake
> risk, but would significantly reduce the livability of our
> homes. Or we could build "disposable" buildings,
> intended to be replaced after the first damaging
> earthquake. The answer lies somewhere between these
> extremes, and the Commission believes the question
> must be answered at a policy level before building codes
> and state law can adequately address the practical issues
> of improving buildings.[9]

California is by no means alone on the front line of the conflict
in seismic safety. In California, the certainty is there that
significant earthquakes will occur. In other regions, the added
uncertainty as to whether a significant earthquake is even on
the horizon bedevils design judgment. New York City, for
example, now has a seismic code, but the probability of even a
moderate earthquake in that vicinity is low. The burden of the
code on new building design is probably negligible, but not so
with existing buildings in the event of a major remodeling. Will
these new code provisions be taken seriously in such instances,
or will hardship applications rule the day?

The Wasatch Front in Utah is a seismically active region.
Like New York City, it is also one of great uncertainty, not so
much in terms of the likelihood of an earthquake, but in terms
of its probable intensity. A 1993 effort by the Uniform
Building Code Commission of Utah to add a Seismic Zone 4
(the most stringent) to the state was overturned by the
International Council of Building Officials due to lack of

144

sufficient supporting data.[10] But collected data suggests that accelerations in excess of those called for in Seismic Zone 3 are likely to occur in heavily populated areas.[11] Indeed, the ground conditions in much of the Salt Lake and Ogden valleys—deep alluvial soils with high water tables—are ideal for seismic wave magnification and for the possibility of extremely strong shear forces in the natural frequencies of medium and tall buildings being unleashed in the case of a major seismic event. Although substantial opinion disagreed with the ruling in Utah, substantial opinion supported it as well. Lack of consensus over the actual level of seismic hazard threatens to derail designers' dependence on conventions and widespread agreement as the ethical basis for their actions.

Designers of Utah's buildings, then, face many of the same dilemmas outlined above. Should they decide that the current code inadequately protects against the hazards raised by potential earthquakes, they must deliberate over whether to conform to conventional expectations or craft a more personal ethic in matters of seismic performance. Lack of consensus makes it impossible for many designers, and for the profession at large, to do the right thing. The choice between violating the client's trust or the potential well-being of the public is intolerable from a moral perspective; a moral precept will fall by the wayside, no matter which course a designer takes.

A clear public mandate would alleviate the problem of designing for the Wasatch Front, as it would the discrepancy between public expectations and code targets in California. It is curious, therefore, that no one appears to have ever tried to determine the level of building performance and seismic safety for which the public is willing to pay. Design professionals treat public interest in a paternalistic fashion, creating no opportunity to assess whether the code represents the public interest. This calls into question the professionals'

145

ability to keep up their side of the pact with the public, and it complicates the task of assembling an ethical theory to inform one's views. Do engineers and architects try to interpret the public interest and act accordingly, or do they act according to their personal notions of professional duty? If they choose the former, then the design professions are doing a poor job of discerning the public interest, and if they choose the latter, then on what basis do they derive these personal notions of duty? If professional duty comes from a commitment to improving one's professional work and the profession's standards, how does one balance the incommensurable interests at work when designing a structure? Interests of economy, safety, and artistry rarely if ever work together. More typically, they tug in opposite directions. The design professional's task is to somehow resolve these interests in a building's design. Explaining one's design decisions by making reference to "professional conscience" is simply not good enough. From what does "professional conscience" derive, if not from the commitment to serve and protect the public as it wishes to be served and protected?

INNER CONFLICT AND THE CODE

In the absence of a strong public imperative, the structural designer must look elsewhere for guidance in designing and improving structures to withstand earthquakes. He or she can let someone else, such as a client or building inspector, make the decisions, thus abdicating his or her own decision-making role; find a way to better ascertain public needs; or use his or her own values as the basis for acting. Though plenty of role-abdication occurs, it is a rare commission indeed that permits the designer no discretion whatsoever. The designer must often craft a personal attitude toward the building code.

But even this mild initiative may be fraught with problems, should the design professional find his personal attitude straying very far from the mainstream of the profession. After all, if each practitioner had substantially different ideas about what was and wasn't adequate, the profession would soon lose all cohesion.

Accepting the code without reservation would allow the designer to push these evaluation issues off onto someone else. Clients and building officials often seem to want to take over the decision-making, but this can hardly be a tenable scenario. Fully rejecting the code as inadequate also quickly dispenses with value issues, by substituting the individual's pre-established values for those established by code-amending processes. This begs the questions, however, of how the code could be in such a sorry state and whether personal judgment has lapsed into arrogance. In the middle ground is where the most immediate ethical dilemmas are found. These dilemmas can be solved by better empirical information, but in the absence of such information, the structural designer is left to his or her own judgment. What sort of theory about professional deliberations and actions can be assembled which would tie these judgments together?

Moral theory offers little help on this point. Resolving conflicts in values is situational; the professional is dedicated to making each situation turn out for the good. Therefore, the situation, not the method, takes precedence. A method for making moral decisions holds only as long as subsequent situations resemble those already encountered. This leaves design professionals without a reliable method for resolving design issues that involve an ethical dilemma. They are obliged to proceed by using judgment (a vague concept) and intuition based on experience (another vague concept) and are likely to experience a degree of inner conflict over the right

147

course of action.[12] The public has, in effect, made the professional its repository for certain dilemmas requiring the combination of basic values with highly technical knowledge, but the professional has a vested interest in keeping such ethical deliberations to a minimum.[13] The obvious solution to the problem of method in ethical dilemmas of seismic design is to eliminate as many value decisions as possible from the process. The function of empirical data-gathering is to take the decision out of the ethical domain and place it into the much more manageable domain of technique.

THE RETROFIT DILEMMA

As fraught with pitfalls as is interpreting the seismic code for new construction, the structural design profession appears to be at least reasonably unified in its approach. The survey suggests, however, that even this much cannot be said when it comes to the matter of retrofitting existing buildings. Dilemmas unique to upgrades include the question of whether lower standards for existing buildings are tolerable and if so, how much lower; whether something more than the mitigation of a potential disaster can be derived from the seismic upgrade of a dangerous building; how quickly decision-makers must react to an existing seismic hazard; and finally, how the artistic integrity of the existing building should be addressed. These dilemmas combine to make the upgrade question the most murky of all. Professional or public consensus is lacking, and without such consensus the practitioner's moral reasoning is likely to become substantially abstracted from the problems at hand.

As developmental psychologist Lawrence Kohlberg so aptly demonstrated, all moral decisions are not created equal.[14] Some decisions draw on such basic moral concepts as fear of loss, reciprocity, and group identification. Kohlberg called these concepts conventional, because they rely on relatively well-established community conventions for their operations. Conventional moral reasoning does not involve the actor in questioning what is asked of him. What Kohlberg termed postconventional reasoning, on the other hand, does; the actor is required to question the propriety of his role in things. Kohlberg called this kind of moral evaluation principled reasoning. A clear correspondence between the actor's beliefs and those of his community cannot be counted upon when one engages in this kind of reasoning. Postconventional moral thinking, or principled reasoning, may take the actor much farther afield, engage issues that may at first seem only tangential to the problem at hand, and ultimately be the cause of considerable discomfort. It is often what is called for in the uncomfortable situation of seismic retrofit.

Kohlberg's hierarchy of different types of moral reasoning has come under attack, most notably from social psychologist Carol Gilligan, for the preference it implies for post-conventional reasoning over other modes of moral reflection and decision-making. Gilligan's argument is that Kohlberg's hierarchy reveals a patriarchal preference for such abstract concepts as justice over more maternal conceptions such as caring. This, she says, is gender bias masquerading as objectivity.[15] Kohlberg's reply to this critique is to assert that the higher levels of moral reasoning are simply more adequate; they can engage in considerations that lower levels simply cannot fathom.[16] The ethical dilemmas of seismic design, however, suggest a further rebuff of Kohlberg on this issue. The indispensability of conventions in being able to act ethically as a seismic structural designer would suggest that the type of moral reasoning that places high regard for the norms of one's community is absolutely essential for the principled modes to function at all. Conventional reasoning, then, is the preferred

149

mode whenever possible and is the foundation for more abstract and radical modes of moral reflection. These modes should be engaged in only reluctantly in the situation at hand and only as a result of a breakdown in conventions. Structural designers are much better served by shoring up the conventions of practice through data-gathering and consensus-building than they are by engaging in Kohlbergian principled reasoning. Indeed, it is hard to see how a structural designer could persist very long in the principled mode. Without reassurance from the activities of one's peers and in the absence of public consensus, the structural designer loses touch with the bases for professionalism. If the case of seismic design is any indication, the idea of the individual fighting his own demons and standing up for what is right in the face of a howling rabble has a certain glamour, but it doesn't quite hold up under scrutiny. Most of us would prefer structural designers who share the same crystal-clear idea of failure with the public over designers who have their own unusual ideas on the subject.

This is not to satirize Kohlberg's point of view, but to question the validity of his hierarchy. It may well be that one is unable to attain the principled level of reasoning without passing through others, but this does not automatically make more abstract moral reasoning any more fit for a given task. The problem with questioning conventions is not the questioning itself, but the inability to fully anticipate the repercussions of one's actions. Reasoning and rationality are fine as far as they go, but one should be wary of letting them carry the actor too far from the known. Conventions play a crucial role. While they do work to constrict the field of possible actions—a negative in Kohlberg's estimation—they also inform the actor of the likely outcomes. After leaving conventions behind, the space of possible outcomes grows exponentially, making it all but impossible to anticipate the

150

results of one's actions. Such unpredictability may lead to some unfortunate results in the aesthetic realm, but it can lead to disastrous results in structural design. Society is right to be wary of novel structural solutions.

UTILITARIANISM AND FIRMITAS

As suggested earlier, large areas exist in architectural design that do not conform well to deliberation over the consequences of conflicting design strategies. Some areas, however, do lend themselves to such deliberations. Structural design is, for the most part, one of those areas. The practice of optimizing the benefits while minimizing the liabilities works well most of the time; architects and engineers do not often push the envelope beyond widely agreed-upon ends and well-understood means. Except for those practitioners charged with actually determining the content of the building code, performance standards, and the like, the ends are usually well-defined in advance. These ends enjoy society's widespread acquiescence. This makes consequentialist, or utilitarian, thinking ideally suited for structural designers. In seismic design situations, however, that envelope is tested. Other means of determining the correct way to proceed are needed. This need is typically glossed over by utilitarian philosophers, who generally cast the problem of determining the right thing to do as something that is available to anyone of average intelligence and access to relevant information, if only they are willing to take a hard look at the problem from impartial eyes.[17] These particular examples of structural design suggest instead that important situations occur in which the amount of information needed to make a decision based on consequences simply does not exist.

    Structural designers generally conceive of their roles as being concerned with means, not ends. Their deliberations are

151

concerned with ends. The problems involved with interpreting the seismic code and with arriving at a consensus about seismic upgrade indicate that utilitarian thinking—often championed as the one form of ethical deliberation that does not shy away from the hard questions—can be derailed in situations in which the desired ends are vague or the fit between society's expectations and engineering performance goals is poor. To be motivating and convincing, consequential thinking depends on both clearly established social norms and specific ends. When these norms and ends are unavailable, practitioners must look elsewhere for justification of their decisions. Structural designers, understandably, avoid such situations. Yet, in certain areas of seismic design, their existence deserves to be acknowledged. In the work of establishing both ends and means, consequential thinking alone is not up to the task.

In the face of a failure of technical knowledge, a significantly higher factor of safety needs to be employed. This would undoubtedly raise the cost of building, but it stands to establish a level of confidence for designers and those affected by their designs so that design may proceed without renewed dilemmas. The seismic code already contains certain measures that reflect the problems of uncertainty. By requiring certain crucial buildings—hospitals, fire stations, emergency control centers—to withstand higher levels of seismic force, the code recognizes an undesirable element of risk in the standard provisions. This concept might be expanded to cover more design situations.

Another side constraint currently employed in many California communities, is to place a time limitation on the upgrade of unreinforced masonry buildings (UMBs). Buildings not upgraded to a certain (relatively low) standard by a certain date stand to be demolished. This places a constraint on utilitarian design thinking by threatening to take a summary action should an uncaring attitude be perceived on the part of the owners of hazardous buildings. This time limitation requires building owners to adopt an air of urgency perceived by local communities. In the case of UMBs, the hazard to the public is perceived as sufficiently high that any hardship incurred by the building owners is given lower priority.

Despite the appeal of such side constraints in individual cases, some worry that their introduction into design deliberations brings with it an element of irrationality. In the case of UMBs, society must cast the owners of hazardous buildings as the transgressors, rather than as innocent victims of owning such structures, to justify demolishing these buildings. (Otherwise, society would find ways to buy their property, as is does in road construction. But why should these building owners be seen as transgressors?) For the most part, they neither built these buildings themselves, nor did they know of the hazard when they purchased them. In a very real sense, they are victims of this situation as well. In the case of the failure of empirically derived evidence to the contrary, the apparent irrationality of requiring higher standards lies in escalating construction costs in the face of no proven benefit. The existing standards may be adequate, but it may equally be the case that they are not.[18]

In seeking to find a reasonable middle ground between the apparent irrationalism of side constraints and the problems that derail consequentialist thinking, philosopher J. L. Mackie proposes a system of *prima facie* rights—rights that are balanced against one another by appeal not to consequences, but to equality of sacrifice. The right to safe buildings, for example, or the right not to be hit by crumbling bricks, might be maintained. This way of thinking bypasses the need to talk in terms of victims and agents, while still considering morality to be a matter of protecting individuals. To avoid the irrationality of absolute rights leading to circumstances less desirable than discarding such rights, Mackie's rights would not be absolute, but *prima facie*; that is, it would be assumed that conflicts, reconsiderations, and restraints of various kinds would be operating on these rights.[19]

Utilitarians question why the notion of *prima facie* rights cannot be accounted for in terms of consequences.[20] Indeed, once one ceases to think of rights as absolute, the distinction between rights-based moralities and consequential-based moralities becomes blurred. For our purposes, we would not know whether to advocate such a right as the right to safe buildings until we knew what was meant by the phrase safe building, and it is highly likely that the phrase will be defined in terms of certain performance criteria that attempt to optimize benefits while minimizing costs. A safe building is likely to be one that, under all but extreme circumstances, provides shelter and certain amenities for its inhabitants. Determining what these extreme circumstances are and how to provide shelter until such events transpire is, of course, the problem facing seismic designers at the outset. Thus, nothing will have been achieved by this roundabout reasoning, which discards one set of consequences only to pick up another.

Against this circularity, at least one moral philosopher would invite structural designers to stop looking at "maximizing the good" and "not maximizing the good" as poles between which ethical deliberation must sway. Rather, Philippa Foot would advocate "maximizing" as the result of thinking through the virtue of benevolence.[21] Once one begins to look inward for ethical motivations, rather than outward for impartial measures of relative good outcomes, the problem of derailed consequential thinking and of attempts to redirect such an outlook back towards beneficial results can be seen as only one aspect of morality. Although the virtue of benevolence

154

is outcome-oriented, other virtues, such as kindness, are not. One is kind because one prefers to be kind, not for what this way of behaving may, in turn, lead to. Once one begins to accept that not all of our moral motivations are outcome-oriented, the logjam brought on by the failure of optimization stands to be broken.

This invitation to look inward when the possibilities of looking outward are exhausted is not new to this discussion. Anderson's expressive theory, discussed in chapter three, recommends such an idea. Such "recontextualizing" moves should be familiar fodder for architects. Recontextualizing design problems is often used as a means of finding new ways to address them. Horst Rittel's concept of the wicked problem shows this inherent similarity between the moral dilemma and the design problem: both can be endlessly recontextualized as symptoms of other problems.[22]

What does this invitation to look inward achieve for the stymied structural designer? When the project of maximizing the good collapses, several other projects fall into the void. Specifically, the project of regarding the opinion of the agent (in this case, the designer) to count for no more than one opinion among many collapses. This is due to the fact that when circumstances reach this point, designers are simply no longer able to formulate an impartial point of view; referencing one's own point of view is all that is left. This development places the wants, opinions, beliefs, and motivations of the designer at the fore. In order for this development not to degenerate into simple egoism, the designer must accept a higher obligation for his or her acts.[22]

In utilitarian calculations, the agent enjoys a certain anonymity, morally speaking, for considering everyone's views as equally relevant as one's own. As the self becomes increasingly involved, however, the agent becomes increasingly

155

responsible for justifying not only his or her decisions, as in consequentialist thinking, but also for his or her preferences and motivations—things for which the utilitarians are largely off the hook. The designer's own views become increasingly relevant. One can, of course, proceed according to what gives one personal pleasure, or according to power politics; but one can also proceed according to a conception of virtue, such as courage, kindness, or compassion. The actions emanating from these character traits may not, in the end, result in maximizing the good, but the agent accepts a higher degree of responsibility for this outcome than that required of the utilitarian, who often takes refuge in the disclaimer that he or she did the best with what they had at hand. When a conception of the self has been included in one's deliberations, a negative outcome hits closer to home. There would seem to be no way of distancing oneself from failure in the way that the utilitarian can. While this approach to moral reasoning does not guarantee a positive result, it does, at least, embody a sense of fairness lacking in the utilitarian approach by balancing increased self-awareness against increased responsibility.

The durability and performance of a building is always more dependent upon empirical research for its methods and ends than are its utility and aesthetic merit. Empirical inquiry will eventually take seismic design out of the realm of the ethical and place it in the realm of technique. Society has a stake in this development coming to pass. The building code, at its best, is the summation of all this empirical data-gathering put into a format both easily interpreted and applied. At its worst, it embodies a series of educated guesses that combine into conservative strategies sufficient to keep the designer out of trouble. Where the seismic code actually lies within this continuum is a matter of opinion.

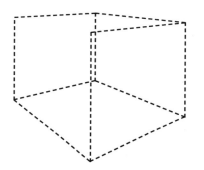

CHAPTER 6 | CONTEXT

Architecture is the most context-sensitive of the arts, so much so that the ennobling of architecture's context is often considered one of its basic values. Given the importance of context in design deliberations and the esteem with which the most successful context-sensitive buildings are held—think of Frank Lloyd Wright's Fallingwater, for instance, or of Jørn Utzon's Sydney Opera House—it is perplexing to find that modern buildings so often make poor neighbors in established urban environments. This criticism is so characteristic of modern architecture that not a few communities have taken the extraordinary step of actually legislating against this style of building. The values that gird a modernist outlook—an emphasis on maintaining a critical stance toward the styles that preceded it, a belief in the transcendent power of the creative design solution, distrust of bourgeois conventions, an embrace of the new, a preference for the universal and immutable over the local and contingent, and a predilection for regarding everything from a functional standpoint—provide the best explanation for this perplexing situation. Postmodernism, traditionalism, historicism, and environmental- and social-activist movements have all contributed formidable critiques of modernism's unsympathetic attitude toward pre-modern buildings and urban patterns.

The spread of skyscraper cities across the Pacific Rim is only the latest instance of modern architecture's difficulties in this regard. Modernist office towers, convention halls, and hotels are rising throughout Asia willy-nilly, in what only yesterday were traditionally organized neighborhoods. Critics of this trend worry that the integrity of harmonious environments is being permanently rent by Western-style modernism. The style, use patterns, and sizes of modern buildings in Taipei, Kuala Lumpur, Shanghai, Bangkok, and elsewhere introduce too many antagonistic elements into the urban fabric for it to survive unscathed. While many critics of Asia's headlong dash into the creation of skyscraper cities cite the social problems created by the pressures on traffic, sanitation, noise, and the like, another branch of the discussion centers on the contextual inappropriateness of these new developments. These modern buildings introduce discordant materials, forms, and scale into previously harmonious environments. Hong Kong architect Nelson Chen's asserts,

> It's amazing how quickly hundreds or even thousands of years of environmental compatibility can get wiped out. . . . The preoccupation with Western-style architecture has resulted in an architectural Chernobyl—an uncontrolled fallout of conflicting building styles and contradictory land uses.[1]

The concern of critics such as Chen is that the context will be appreciated only after it has been lost.

This renewed sensitivity to context occurs at a time when the built environment in the United States is losing much of its sense of place. In his *Variations on a Theme Park*, Michael Sorkin identifies three important trends occurring in urban America that are harming the quality of our urban environments: ageographia, in which the physical form of one location is repeated in another; increased surveillance and control; and the creation of endless simulations. The dissemination of modernist values has had a hand in the first of these trends. One of modernism's tenets, after all, is a universally applicable, rational approach to design. Sorkin explains,

> The new city . . . eradicates genuine particularity in favor of a continuous urban field, a conceptual grid of boundless reach. . . . In this vast, virtually undifferenti-ated territory—stretching from Fairfax County, Virginia to Orange County, California—homes, offices, factories, and shopping malls float in a culturing medium, a "non-place urban realm" that provides the bare functions of a city while doing away with the vital, not quite disciplined formal and social mix that gives cities life.[2]

These sentiments, embedded though they are in sensible observation, rely on the broad assumption that context is something that, when accurately described, leads to conclusions about its value. This assumption, however, leads to certain weaknesses in the arguments by critics of modernism's tendency toward universalization. It would seem obvious to a critic like Chen that the context for the modern buildings that have infiltrated Shanghai is the urban pattern and buildings of the old colonial city. But, of course, this would not be considered the relevant context by Shanghai's planners, developers, and architects. For them, the context would be China's emergence as a major world trading partner.

For Sorkin, the relevant context for Orange County would be Southern California, with its inimical climate and Spanish history; for Fairfax County, a former British colony with real winters. But for the upwardly mobile population that may find itself moving back and forth between these two places, the similarities may outweigh the differences. The difficulty comes in establishing by reasonably objective standards just what the essentials of a particular location's context are.

Modernists unapologetically maintain that globalization, scientific rationality, and technology are the most important elements of any context in this day and age; climate, history, and topography must be dealt with, of course, but they are easily dispatched. This attitude, simply put, is what it means to be modern. For modernism's critics, however, a notion of context is not so easily formulated. One can make a list of important contextual considerations, including climate, topography, local building practices, history, and cultural patterns, but one's decision to call a halt to the list is a normative one. No objective means exist to determine which criteria are relevant and which are not. One can avoid this dilemma by claiming, in effect, "Context is everything you can think of," but this is a horrible abdication, given that humans are limited beings and that some sort of prioritizing must occur for judgment to proceed. One can only describe context by first bracketing the terms with a value judgment. Holding context to have normative content helps bolster the idea that context is one of the goods of architecture.

Rather than accept the completely normative character of context, one could limit the factors that make up context to those that are likely to go uncontested. Every location has a climate that is either relatively comfortable or relatively harsh for human habitation, and certain imperatives flow from this observation. Every location has a certain topography, as well. The problem with taking this course, however, is that it woefully underdetermines the design judgments to follow. With so many products of technology available to mitigate and modify the found environment, climate and topography simply fail to fully account for form. One could take the attitude, as certain environmentalists do, that we should let climate rule our decisions to a greater extent than is typically allowed, but this course once again introduces the value judgment at the beginning of design deliberations, rather than at the conclusion, as the critics would prefer. While a modernist outlook is up-front about starting from a certain set of value judgments, its critics—who wish judgment to follow from observation—must vacillate between arbitrariness and underdetermination.

This same problem undermines Kenneth Frampton's notion of "critical regionalism," an idea posited to provide an alternative to the oppressive universalizing tendencies of modernism, the lack of integrity in neo-historicism, and the mannerism of the avant-garde. "Regionalism," Frampton asserts, is a "way of building sensitive to the vicissitudes of time and climate."[3] Frampton attempts to ground his regionalism in something more fundamental than style and surface effects, but the content of his notion is elusive. He develops criteria to distinguish critical regionalism from the universalizing tendencies of modernism on the one hand, and from the sentimental surface effects of historicism on the other hand. Only the criterion that "Critical Regionalism favours the realization of architecture as a tectonic fact rather than the reduction of the built environment to a series of ill-assorted scenographic episodes" could be employed to discredit phenomena such as "Santa Fake" pseudo-adobe design in New Mexico. We might well ask, however, whether "Santa Fake" fails to make the grade because it does not use true adobe tectonics, or because it emulates an antiquated and therefore not sufficiently modern technology? "Santa Fake" arguably persists precisely because it is critical of mainstream modernism. It co-opts as much modern technology as it needs to build efficiently and still maintain its critical distance from modernism. Indeed, none of the locals actually fool themselves into thinking that what they are looking at is true adobe. They are, instead, invoking a spirit of resistance and community. To dismiss "Santa Fake" for its sentimentality is to miss the point.

CHAPTER 6 | CONTEXT

By the measure of regionalism, Chicago—the birthplace of the skyscraper—would arguably be the only city deserving of sleek, exciting, tall buildings. This narrow attitude can be avoided, but then the concept of regionalism loses all capacity to support normative distinctions. If modern skyscrapers are considered regionally appropriate in cities with vibrant skylines such as New York and Hong Kong, why can't they become regionally appropriate in Shanghai? If we follow the temptation to admit that skyscrapers can become regionally appropriate in Shanghai under certain conditions, then theories of regionalism fall apart altogether. Either one takes a theoretical stand against allowing modernistic skyscrapers in certain locations no matter what, or admits that this theory is not ultimately about location, but about satisfying certain conditions: social utility, perhaps, or ecological concerns. Against regionalism, modernism and westernization would seem to have proven decisively that skyscrapers can be built anywhere on the globe, that a mainstream modernist outlook can become part of the culture of Caracas, Johannesburg, and Tokyo, just as easily as it can of Chicago. This is due to the power of modernism's universalist pretensions, embedded in a similarly universalist, utilitarian morality. Modernism, in this sense, is an intrepid traveler, ready to make itself at home anywhere.

Critics of modernism's universalizing tendencies might well counter that modernism's moral underpinnings have been sufficiently discredited by postmodernists, traditionalists, historicists, feminists, and environmentalists that it no longer matters whether opposing theories of contextual appropriateness are somewhat muddled; it is enough to say that the modern approach simply does not work. Proponents of modernism may even agree with its critics that the heroic ideals of revolutionizing the world through architecture are passé. But modernism's shortcomings are no more glaring than those of its

164

critics. A postmodern outlook may be more ameliorative toward existing urban environments, and its embrace of value pluralism may result in an urbanism that provides environments superior to those generated by modernist precepts, but postmodernism's separation of the functional and the aesthetic, coupled with its vacillation between popular and prudential preferences, leaves many practitioners cold. Traditionalists, on the other hand, may minimize the break with the past, which occurred in the wake of the remarkable technological and social developments of the last century, but they settle too easily for preciousness, rather than demanding integrity. Historicists champion integrity but tend to suspend the commonsense perception that all contexts are not created equal. They often seem to place great importance on the preservation of insignificant remnants, thus perpetuating the conflict between maintaining the integrity of the past and that of the present. Environmentalists place the environmental modifications of the past and the present on equal footing—and regard them with equal suspicion. They presume that a guilty conscience should be the starting point of one's deliberations, at least in all Western liberal democracies. Social activists do not single out the Western world for criticism, but like environmentalists, they encourage a myopic instrumentalism that diminishes one's ability to actually care about beautiful buildings at all. Each approach raises a legitimate issue. Those issues, however, do not easily combine into a single, unified theory.

The assumption that context can be described objectively is at the bottom of the critics' difficulties in sustaining a run against the ruination of urban settings by modernist buildings. We would be better served by dropping this assumption—the last vestiges of a discredited ideology—and assuming instead that context is, like *utilitas, firmitas*, and *venustas*, a thick concept, which marries fact and value in a single idea.[4] The notion of context has no content without a normative component. Context cannot be described; it must be justified. To speak of a context as something that exists from any rational point of view—or all rational points of view—is to throw one's hand in to the universalists. The modernists would then have the discussion exactly where they want it, discussing relative benefits and liabilities rather than right and wrong. The critic can circumvent this discussion by avoiding the temptation to think in terms of "the context," substituting in its place "our context," or "their context." It then becomes the modernist's decision whether to join "us" or not.[5]

What follows, then, from taking up the notion that to have any content, context presumes a moral community? Does it make any practical difference? Does it lead to more difficulties than it explains? Do any of the competing architectural theories or critiques—functionalism, historicism, social activism, the aesthetic—enjoy an advantage over the others in this regard?

THE SALK CONTROVERSY

The implications of the functionalist and aesthetic points of view can be put to the test through an examination of Louis Kahn's Salk Institute in La Jolla, California, and of the controversy surrounding the recent addition to the building. With the prospect of the addition, the contextual integrity of one of the greatest works of twentieth-century architecture hung in the balance.

Admiration for the Louis Kahn's Salk Institute, especially among architects, has slowly grown from the time of its initial occupation in 1965 to its induction by the 1990s into the pantheon of great twentieth-century architecture. This heightened esteem was not the result of any subsequent changes made to the place itself; indeed, virtually the only changes that occurred during the Salk's first thirty years were the ceaseless remodeling of its laboratory spaces, the gradual development of the property around the once isolated site, and the inexorable growth of a grove of eucalyptus trees planted along the institute's eastern boundary.

Appreciation for the Salk was largely the result of a growing appreciation for the role of Louis Kahn in the turn away from the strictures of International Style architecture—a turn that allowed postmodernism and other tendencies to bloom. This is not to reduce Kahn's artistic achievement to something of mere historical importance. On the contrary, the Salk continues to impress contemporary designers. When Jonas Salk decided the time was right to build a long-contemplated administration building, he made every effort to respect Kahn's original conception of the project. He contacted two of the architects who had actually worked with Kahn on the original buildings, and the scheme they developed closely followed certain drawings by Kahn, which proposed adding a building on the east end of the plaza, perpendicular to the existing buildings. This scheme would, in effect, create a new terminus to the eastern edge of the campus. To build it, the eucalyptus grove through which visitors wended their way from the parking lot to the plaza would have to be mowed down. In deference to Kahn, however, the addition would touch neither the existing buildings, nor the plaza, and would instead be freestanding.

Although the Salk has many admirable qualities (the clarity of use expressed through form, the high quality of its concrete work, the ingenuity of its planning), the thing that really excites people—the element that architects come from all over the world to see—is the plaza. Paved entirely in travertine, the plaza is bounded on the north and south sides by the research labs and split down the middle by a narrow stream of water. The space is in part so successful because of the unconventional way it is enclosed. The west side of the campus opens onto the Pacific Ocean and is not terminated at all; the paving simply stops, the water channel falls, and all is inflected toward the infinite horizon. On the east side, the green-gray curtain of eucalyptus provides just enough enclosure to obscure the mundane world of parking lots and roads, but not so much as to create a visual hierarchy leading from east to west. Reinforced by the water channel, the east-west axis appears infinitely long—more like an extrusion than a courtyard or town square. At the Salk, Kahn created a new type of outdoor space, and he created a good one—even a great one.

The artistic triumph Kahn achieved in the plaza was a fragile matter. Any alteration, such as cutting down the eucalyptus grove, was likely to alter things. When the proposed addition to the Salk was first unveiled by the San Francisco architectural firm Anshen + Allen in 1991, it quickly became a matter of controversy within the profession. The positions taken on the Salk addition fell into three categories: one based on an appreciation of what Salk intended for the site, one based on notions of the building's functionality, and a third grounded in aesthetic values. By examining the ideas that informed these three positions, some conclusions about context as a source of architectural value can be made.

THE HISTORICAL ARGUMENT

Brian Henderson, president of the Salk Institute, defended the Anshen + Allen design, which placed a partially submerged administration building at the eastern edge of the plaza and bifurcated it to allow for the extension of the east-west axis. He called it "historically based and the most functionally appropriate solution."[6] What Henderson meant by "historically based" was that this location was identified by both Kahn and Salk as the place for the administration building.[7] If Kahn wanted the design to evolve in this way, and if it was his vision that lead to the artistic success of the place, then it seems only right that the addition should take this form.

This historicist approach pays deference to the history of Kahn's original design and to the development of the site from its earliest beginnings, as recorded in conversations, sketches, and plans. During the present-day design deliberations, these became important archeological resources. The current proposal was regarded as the completion of a fundamental component of the project as previously designed. The motivation behind the historical argument is, however, unclear: does it turn on a certain reverence for Kahn, claiming simply, "This was the intention of the great Louis Kahn and we want to instantiate that vision"? Or, does it make the more complex evaluation, "This was the vision of the great Louis Kahn, and upon reflection we think it was a good vision, so this is what we want to do"? The former avoids any critical evaluation of what has come before, while the latter claims to make one. The former makes only one value judgment, that Kahn's intentions are paramount. The designer only attempts to stay as faithful as possible to the artifacts he or she has at hand. This approach is meek, but uncomplicated. The second possible motivation— that Kahn's original design is inherently valuable and worthy of pursuing—constitutes a stronger stance, but it raises the question of what other options were considered. Presumably, the decision-makers entertained all the other plausible ideas before concluding that Kahn's own placement of the administration building was the best design solution.

Henderson's comments about the Anshen + Allen scheme indicate that the institute was not content to simply espouse a

169

blind allegiance to Kahn. They also felt compelled to bolster their argument by maintaining the functional superiority of the proposed addition. If the historical argument does not silence the critics, throw in an appeal to function. Suddenly, the humble desire to defer to the artistic vision of an acknowledged master begins to look more like an excuse for the exercise of will, if not ego. This is perfectly acceptable, if one is willing to baldly declare that the decision was made out of personal preference, rather than some alleged appeal to the best outcome from an ethical point of view. The meeker response, which blindly respects Kahn's intentions, is actually the only internally consistent option in this instance.

Some have argued that, regardless of a few sketches, Kahn was hardly of a set mind in the matter.[8] The record of the design process of the original Salk is a tale of last minute redesigns and the dragging on of undecided issues of major importance.[9] Indeed, the character of the plaza itself was decided very late in the project, after construction had begun, and only then with the strong nudging of the great Mexican architect Luis Barragán. Stanford Anderson was concerned that the addition to the Salk would be

> completely contrary to north-south continuity in that such an administration building would finally solidify the symmetry of the laboratories and the entire site. . . . Whatever qualities such an environment may have, it is clearly completely opposed to Kahn's original form-idea for the Salk Institute.[10]

Yet, perhaps this does not matter too much. The sketches are there, they are Kahn's, and they substantiate the fact that Kahn gave this issue much more thought than anyone who came later.

Failing to consider intentions when making design decisions impoverishes the thought process. This observation, however, referred to the current designer's own intentions, not

170

to the intentions of someone long dead. What is to be gained from maintaining that Kahn's intentions are paramount in the face of a loud chorus of knowledgeable detractors? Fidelity to the original vision is one benefit. Like the problem of artistic forgery, a person would often rather have a second rate original by a master than a first rate imitation by someone else. This emphasizes the value of participating in an acknowledged master's vision. This is not a novel idea in architecture. Posthumously constructed works designed by Aalto and Wright have been executed with as much fidelity as possible to what the great architects left behind.[11] Indeed, one of Kahn's unbuilt projects was created on the computer, so that at least a virtual three-dimensional version of it could be seen and experienced.[12] Part of the value of these works transcends the individual artistic accomplishment each building represents. Their value is also in the their being part of the larger body of work of Wright, and Aalto, and Kahn.

This value should not be dismissed as meaningful only to the disciple of a great master. No artist creates magnificent work at every outing—not Wright, not Picasso, not Beethoven, and certainly not Kahn. This realization, however, does not lead us to conclude that the world would be better off without their mediocre works. Rather, the world is better off with their mediocre works in it, not only because a mediocre Picasso is probably better than the best work of a great many other artists, but also because even the artist's worst moments help inform and educate contemporary artists. The same goes for Kahn. This esteem, however, can only be claimed for a handful of recognized masters in their disciplines. It would make no sense to hold up for esteem the works of architects who have made no notable contribution to the course of their art. But Kahn is widely held to be a master, not a member of the rank and file, and the Salk is one of the reasons.

The historicist point of view carries weight. It is simple, consistent, and backed by precedent. It does, however, contain a significant bias that deserves investigation. The historicist approach places a certain value on humility, on the architect's suppressing his or her own will and acting in accordance with a sense of duty to someone else's vision. The dependence of the historicist point of view on Kantian ethics, it turns out, is great. Kant would have us act not out of consideration for the consequences of one's actions but out of devotion to the universal laws of morality, which ultimately translates into acting for the sake of duty itself. Kant thought this strong turn is necessary because in practical deliberations over the consequences of one's actions the ego necessarily interferes. He writes about "the dear self," which is "always turning up; and it is on this that the purpose of our actions is based—not on the strict command of duty, which would often require self-denial."[13] To the extent that the ego surfaces, the probability of acting ethically diminishes. Kant uses this observation to support the conclusion that principles of morality, of right action, must be "cleansed of everything that can only be empirical and appropriate to anthropology."[14] He adds,

> [S]uch a completely isolated metaphysic of morals, mixed with no anthropology, no theology, no physics or hyperphysics, still less with occult qualities (which might be called hypophysical), is not only an indispensable substratum of all theoretical and precisely defined knowledge of duties, but is at the same time a desideratum of the utmost importance for the actual execution of moral precepts.[15]

Kant's striving for purity of judgment may strike us as quaint. At the start of the twenty-first century we are more used to striving for ways to enrich the information coming to bear upon our judgments. The lessons of anthropology, social science, and history are increasingly folded into architectural design judgments and ethical deliberations, rather than expunged from them. Certainly, the arguments this discussion has been favoring elsewhere argue for the benefits of inclusive, impure reasoning, as opposed to Kant's purifying approach. Certain benefits of this approach should, however, be acknowledged. By stripping away so many potential reasons for right action, Kant avoids the problems of incommensurability and intuition-based reasoning that complicate the present age. He makes acting ethically a conceptually simple (which is not to say easily achieved) matter. By always appealing to the one thing that is under every circumstance good—the good will—his approach is internally consist.

THE FUNCTIONALIST ARGUMENT

Part of what makes the Salk successful as architecture is that it is a beautiful place where work occurs. Both the demands of *utilitas* and *venustas* are satisfied in generous bucketfuls and this makes the whole experience superior to what it would be if the facility were difficult to use, or used only ceremoniously or occasionally, or no longer used for its intended purpose at all. Some of its architectural value would be lost if a decline in its functionality were to occur. Architecture gains meaning and value through use. That the plaza could be so monumental, so other-worldly, and still be part of a functioning institution favorably informs its critical reception and makes Kahn's achievement all the more worthwhile. A sense of economy also contributes to the building's success. A building that can provide a high degree of both utility and aesthetic pleasure is superior to a simply beautiful or simply functional one. Indeed, part of what singles out the Salk as the triumph that Kahn's earlier project, the Richards Medical Laboratories in

173

Philadelphia, is not is this issue of functionality; to reduce the functional capabilities of the Salk would be to reduce its value as architecture.

This point of view, which values both *utilitas* and *venustas* within a single work of architecture, has a long pedigree in architectural theory, and with good reason. Kahn perhaps took this idea into new territory. Michael Benedikt has suggested that the architect was "committed, as no one else seemed to be, to the all-but-impossible mission of showing how architecture should and could unite the transcendent with the workaday worlds."[16]

Aaron Betsky emphasized the functional as a tonic to the tendency to regard the Salk from a preservationist point of view. He asked, "Is there something sacred about the existing building that needs to be protected against the changes in use that define our experience of architecture?" and concluded that the answer was "no."[17] Deploring the meekness of the historical approach, he would have preferred an architect who "has as problematic a relationship to the nature of institutions and their role in society as Kahn did."[18] Betsky would deflate the reverence or aura surrounding Kahn's achievement:

> I am disturbed by what I believe is the underlying vacu-
> ousness of the worshipers at Kahn's shrine. The Anshen
> + Allen strategy, the opposition to their effort and the
> recent adulation of Kahn on the occasion of the retro-
> spective of his work at MOCA are all symptoms of the
> transformation of this accomplished architect into a
> combination of Yoda and Howard Roark.[19]

What does such a deflation of the mystique surrounding the Salk achieve? Betsky would like us to regard this building, and this design problem, as critically as any other. Following this lead, however, one wonders how the designers could

174

proceed any differently than they would in a less celebrated situation. If one firmly rejects the ideas that following an acknowledged master's lead has any intrinsic value and that certain contexts are too fragile to disturb, then what is left looks much like the standard design method, in which a functional program is developed, several alternatives are generated and evaluated, and one that seems the best fit is chosen. Are we wrong to experience a nagging doubt that bringing the design problem of the Salk addition down to earth as just another instance of maximizing form and function will be adequate to capture the urgency and fragility of the situation? Surely the problem of adding to a sensitive context is more complicated than that.

By disallowing the aesthetic achievement of the Salk Plaza to be sacrosanct, one is implicitly agreeing that the plaza must be measured against function for it to sustain any value at all. This is what ultimately makes stances such as Betsky's functionalist when all is said and done. Though the attempt to bring the discussion down to earth is initially welcome, the only way it can stay on the ground is to insist on the negotiability of everything in exactly the same way as the utilitarians do. Insist that some aspect is non-negotiable and that aspect takes on the aura that this approach sought to discard. Nothing escapes negotiability from a utilitarian perspective: not love, not great art, not even life itself is beyond its calculations. Certainly the esteem in which the Salk's plaza is held is not beyond estimation. If more good can be wrought out of the beautiful but otherwise useless plaza by housing a few more research labs, a social club, and a Starbucks, then that is the right thing to do. That Betsky stops short of suggesting such a calculation may be squeamishness on his part, rather than his having identified a logical resting point.

Requiring that the Salk Plaza be responsive to function operates on just such a slippery slope. The chain of reasoning might easily proceed as follows:

> Failing to make the necessary changes to allow the Salk to continue as an institution would introduce a degradation to the architecture. An obsolete Salk is just not as good a building as a working, vibrant one.

> If the addition needs to be built in such a way as to alter the spatial experience of the plaza, this may be a regrettable but necessary price to pay for a living, rather than a dead, work of architecture.

The important moment in the argument comes when aesthetic value starts to be regarded as a kind of utility. Once we start thinking of aesthetic function, which must be weighed with other functions, the long slide has begun. The problem with this thinking is that aesthetic activity does not conform well to any ordinary notions of function. When all of the supposed functions are wrung out of a work of art, we have still to account for the affection we hold it in, or the intrinsic value we perceive in it. This perception of intrinsic value holds regardless of the social, spiritual, or physiological effects the work can engender. The functionalist approach can only address aesthetic merit by making it something it is not—an instance of function—and by turning the design process in even such celebrated situations as the Salk addition into a prosaic activity.

176

The headline "Genius Betrayed" above a letter by Robert Venturi and Denise Scott Brown published in *Architecture* magazine conveys the sense of urgency and moral outrage that many architects felt about the proposed addition to the Salk. Interestingly enough, however, the "genius" referred to in this headline is not Louis Kahn, but the architecture. As for Kahn's intentions, these were irrelevant. What mattered most was "what's there—an expression of the American view of space," which acknowledges "an order that is incomplete as it accommodates expansion toward eternal frontiers."[20] Venturi, Scott Brown, and others draw a profound experience from this, an experience felt to be both art and transcendent of art, with visions of social and cultural frontiers. The unbroken east-west axis of the complex had immense philosophical, symbolic, social, and artistic importance. Closing up the east end of the plaza would ruin the philosophical basis for appreciating the place.

This argument contains an odd mixture of philosophy and aesthetics. The aesthetic experience would be ruined by eviscerating the philosophy supposedly embodied in the design. Yet, the critics say, it matters not whether Kahn intended this unique philosophy to be the basis for design. What matters is that the design came to be understood and appreciated in this way. Others have said that Kahn was troubled by the lack of public consciousness of American institutions and that the Salk, and especially its plaza, expresses the architect's hopes for the facility's transcending both its immediate programmatic requirements and the segregation of work from the rest of life.[21] This argument, however, seems to suggest that this would be a pleasing but irrelevant event. Venturi, Scott Brown, and their followers want their objection to be made on an artistic basis,

177

but not just on matters internal to art (composition, material, form, and the like), but on the immense amount of meaning that artists and observers can invest in the raw materials of art. As an artistic expression of American democratic ideals, the design of the Salk becomes a matter of great cultural importance. Art and morality are here hopelessly intertwined. Standing in the Salk plaza, "the most significant architectural composition of our century and arguably, of all American architecture," Venturi and Scott Brown experienced hope for a distinctly American vision of space.[22]

The authors claimed to be disputing only a few particulars about the planned addition—its "location and arrangement," which transforms "an American architectural masterpiece . . . into an ordinary, Baroque bore," not the basic idea that the Salk needs enlarging.[23] Venturi and Scott Brown placed paramount value on aesthetic experience. They disdained the historicist view regarding Kahn's intentions and show little interest in the functionalist argument either. The value of the aesthetic-philosophical experience of the plaza is the supreme value. Whether the institute is a bustling hub of scientific research or a vacant shell is significant, but it is of secondary concern.

What ethical outlooks underlie this position? First, there would seem to be moral value in preserving "the most significant architectural composition of our century," if architectural compositions have moral value at all. But why call the Salk a "significant composition," rather than, say, "a great work" or "a magnificent place?" Valuing the Salk as a "significant composition" is an attempt to give an instrumental value to its place in history, either to bolster the value of the building as a work of art or to trump artistic value with something more directly consequential. The argument for

178

"significance" is an attempt to be more analytical than judgmental. This appeal to a "fact" about the Salk attempts to secure broad-based approval that an aesthetic judgment could not. "Significance" is an instrumental concept; it makes no sense to call something "significant" in and of itself. Something can only be significant as or for something else, something it contributes, allows, or does. A "significant composition" has a utilitarian value that "a profound space" may not.

Venturi and Scott Brown's argument in favor of the Salk's "significance" does as much damage as it does good, however. Rather than concentrate on the aesthetic merits of the place, one is now directed to focus on its significance in the history of architecture. Had someone else created this sort of space first, its "significance" would be less. This development is inevitable if one values aesthetic goods instrumentally, for the experiences they engender, rather than as goods in and of themselves. This instrumentalist outlook tends to devalue everything except subjective states of mind: happiness, unhappiness, pleasure, feelings of well-being, and the like. Other things are good only insofar as they contribute to these states of mind. Feeling compelled to add the "significance" argument to an aesthetic judgment shows the degree to which consequentialism unsettles otherwise perfectly sensible sentiments.

Venturi and Scott Brown's argument, simply put, goes too far in its attempts to justify the value of the Salk. The "significance" argument goes as follows:

> The architectural composition of the Salk plaza allows people to engage in an aesthetic adventure by experiencing a space that achieves beauty without resorting to the hierarchical compositions characteristic of the expression of authoritarian power.

The expression of hierarchy is avoided by opening up one end of the space to the horizon, the other to the landscape, and by enclosing the sides with identical forms.

This experience has social, and hence moral, value in addition to artistic value. Furthermore, this particular aesthetic achievement has never been bettered.

This restatement makes plain the distinction between analyzing and appreciating the building. The analysis never fully explains the intensity of feeling or the commitment to the beauty of the place shared by the Salk's admirers. Even in a situation where the authors are clearly passionate about the building, it is impossible to fully express this passion by resorting to instrumental reasoning. Rather than appreciating the Salk for what it is, Venturi and Scott Brown justify their appreciation of the Salk on the basis of what it does.

To assert that the design of the Salk is great because it has social value is to give oneself over to functionalism. Attempts to justify the value of aesthetic experience, however, have been notoriously unsuccessful during this century. This is not to say that experiences do not count: they do. Attempts to deny or alter experiences valued by others have moral import. As anthropologist Clifford Geertz notes, there is no reason to think that an aesthetic experience cannot also concurrently be a social experience.[24] At the Salk, we can marvel at how aesthetic expression was given to location, form, materials, space, work, movement, and societal ideals and with an economy of means woven into a tight fabric. This grand achievement deserves our praise and allegiance. To destroy this, or even lessen it, demands a good reason. The need for a visitors center, auditorium, or additional lab space does not quite qualify as such. Experiential value, therefore, would prevail (at least to some degree) in a functionalist argument.

Perhaps greater social utility could be served by the Salk, however, even at the risk of negatively impacting the aesthetics of the place. If the benefits of subletting part of the plaza to Starbucks, which could potentially assure the success of the complex by subsidizing research or building maintenance costs, exceeds those of the aesthetic experience, then too bad for aesthetics. The proponents of aesthetic value might do better to stay away from this type of argument. Rather, they should stick to emphasizing the Salk's many aesthetic virtues. By demanding that the new addition not diminish the aesthetic value of the complex for spurious reasons, the argument can have moral force without deflecting one's sentiments away from the object that inspired them.

The aesthetic value argument can only hope to gain currency by staying close to a discussion about the object itself and avoiding the temptation to stray into a discussion of utility. Aesthetic value and social utility are best left as examples of a plurality of values, rather than ranked against one another. Venturi and Scott Brown's aesthetic argument implicitly subscribes to value pluralism, but only by acknowledging the irreducibility of artistic value can that argument be sustained. It is true that aesthetic value must still be reconciled against other values, but at least it enters this process on its own terms, not on those of the functionalist. To decide between incommensurable values and to choose between incompatible positions, one can look inward.[25]

181

The historicist, functionalist, and aesthetic points of view—each with their implicit moral underpinnings—are usually brought to bear on design situations in which a sensitive context is at stake. One may always reference the basic and irreducible values of intentions, function, and artistic achievement in deciding how to proceed. According to the themes developed so far, the aesthetic value argument's implicit acknowledgment of value pluralism is likely to lead to the most satisfactory results. The historicists, with their sympathies in the Kantian urge to purify moral value down to the demands of duty, are unable to address either the value of aesthetic experience or the importance of maintaining the Salk as a functioning institution. The functionalists, however, with their roots deeply planted in utilitarianism, can only assess the value of duty and of aesthetic experience in terms of how these things facilitate the greatest good, thus discarding altogether the important sense in which aesthetic goods are valued for their own sake and trampling on the idea that one has certain duties that transcend outcome.

A fully satisfactory design deliberation would acknowledge the incommensurability of certain values that come to bear on the project at hand. While proponents of aesthetic value tried to downplay the relevance of the other points of view at the Salk, they did so within the framework of value pluralism, thus implicitly acknowledging the legitimacy of other sources of value as well. This was not ultimately followed by the Salk Institute. The built scheme—a building on the east end that narrows, but is still bifurcated by the strong east-west axis—was roundly regarded by the architectural press as neither ruining the experience of the plaza, as its critics had feared, nor continuing the sense of profundity and daring embodied in the original. Of the three approaches outlined here, these results suggest that the realized project cleaved most closely to the historical outlook. The actual debate stood to be much richer and more inclusive of different points of view had the pluralism of the values at stake been recognized by the decision-makers. Then, the people involved could have made their decisions, not only on the basis of ideal function as modified by certain historical and aesthetic concerns, but also on the basis of what they wished the new addition to express about their values. The larger basis for evaluation may well have changed the form of what was actually built. Absent a pluralistic outlook, architects are obliged to look on contextual sensitivity as an ameliorative process rather than a source of consideration on equal footing with utility. The decisions leading to the ultimate design of the addition would certainly have been based more on persuasion and less on the naked exercise of authority. From an ethical point of view, one could hardly ask for more; from an aesthetic point of view, at least artistic concerns would have been given full consideration.

The historic and functionalist arguments do not come close to capturing the sense of context sought here. The aesthetic value argument comes closest to expressing the noninstrumental dignity that the critics of modernist functionalism would like to sustain in their championing of the value of context. But this approach does not entirely digest the independent value of context. It lacks a concern for context that entails a consideration of intentions and of how things have come to be as they are. Aesthetic value, at best, looks backward in this way only indirectly—a characteristic aesthetic value shares with functionalism. This suggests that architects would have good reasons for asserting context as a source of value comparable to *utilitas, firmitas,* and *venustas.*

This conclusion, however, falls short of establishing context as a value with the assurance that the Vitruvian values enjoy. Context does not share with the Vitruvian values an interest in what goes on inside a building. The imperatives of context entail a flavor of feeling imposed from the outside, rather than generated by the nature of the design problem itself. What it means to assert that "good architecture creates context" is still a somewhat vague concept, unlike the entirely sensible observation that "good architecture creates beauty" or "utility." These differences make context something of an anomaly in the structure of this discussion and may prevent this source of value from ever fitting comfortably within its overall scheme. What is critical, however, is that the door be left open for the inclusion of this and other contenders for the list of architectural values.

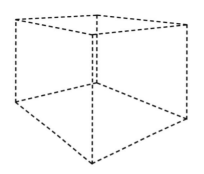

CHAPTER 7 | STYLE

For architects, the word "style" acquired and retains the taint of the provincial in an age excited by universals. Not so for historians. On the concept of style, James Ackerman writes,

> For the artist and for his audience, style is a protection against chaos. It serves the same purpose as do cultural patterns and institutions in society. A class of works of art of any kind—pyramids, portraits of rulers, still lifes—is orderly and distinguishable because it is necessary to human beings not only to express themselves within established patterns; but to experience the world around them in accordance with such patterns; our perceptual mechanisms cause us to interpret what we see in terms of what we know and expect.[1]

The decline in fortune of the concept of style has not come to pass without good reason. For architects wishing to be on the side of timeless beauty, the facile Victorian-era approach to style was intolerable. Modernism promised to provide the sense of conviction lacking in the late nineteenth-century architecture of their predecessors by basing itself on something more fundamental than style. Modernists would derive architectural form from hardheaded, rational deliberation over problems of utility.

To be concerned with more than "mere style," modernists from the outset closely aligned themselves with morality through the doctrine of functionalism. They sought to bridge the distinction between the moral and aesthetic spheres by in essence blurring it. They achieved this by adopting the nineteenth-century version of functionalism worked out by J.-N.-L. Durand—a concept highly dependent on utilitarian modes of thinking.[2] By asserting that utility could, however indirectly, be quantified, modern architects set about determining the most efficient means of providing utility. The functionalist approach was intended to be universally applicable to any design problem because it addressed universal human needs.

Despite widespread repudiation of the value and practicality of deriving expression solely from function, architectural theory has yet to cast off the assumptions of universality underlying the functionalist agenda. The movements arising after modernism's collapse are still its children, in the sense that none have abandoned the ideal of addressing more than "mere style." If "style" was to be embraced at all, it would have to be the International Style. Modernists, postmodernists, and deconstructionists have all rebelled against the idea that the conceptions they were working under constituted a style.[3] They preferred to consider themselves functionalists, rationalists or pluralists, as responding to the "spirit of the age," or as implementing a universal theory of language. Each assumes to have captured a privileged position, to have accessed a deeper truth from which to regard the foibles of others. With postmodernism, this truth is that modernism does not stand outside history, any more than does any other human endeavor. With deconstructionism, this truth is that modernism and postmodernism are captives of an ancient antagonism that must be discarded in order to liberate culture. With neoclassicism, the truth lies in the timelessness of classical principles and motifs.

What would ensue if these movements gave up on the presumption of having captured some universal, timeless truth and accepted instead that each provides only limited insights and limited applicability to culture? Most immediately, proponents of each movement would have to accept the idea that room exists for all to ply their trade. Each would have to acknowledge that he or she holds no privileged position from which to judge others. The deconstructionists would have to embrace the possibility that the postmodern celebration of popular culture is intellectually respectable. The post-modernists would have to accept that a straight, non-ironic revivalism is a viable mode of expression. The neoclassicists would be obliged to look on deconstructed works as something more than the degeneration of culture. Modernists would have to look on all three as something other than eccentricities in its ongoing trajectory. In other words, each movement would have to accept the others for what they say they are, rather than claim to have proven conclusively that the others are intellectually inferior.

To accept one's own incomplete picture of the world is to accept that one will never conclusively prove anything, that one only constructs provisional, fallible, although hopefully durable narratives. Proponents of these theories may be willing to make these concessions to the others, but the even more difficult task that ensues from acknowledging one's limited place in the world is that each proponent of a movement would also have to give up a cherished presumption about his or her own outlook. By discarding universalistic pretensions and accepting that one's favorite mode of architectural expression may have only limited appeal and applicability means that one is, after all, working within a limited set of conventions with recognizable forms and motifs—that is to say, working within a style.

An air of the ignoble pervades the concept of style. Today most architects can only squirm when asked in what style they work. Everyone wants their favored mode of expression, be it modernism, postmodernism, deconstruction, or even classicism, to be about more than "mere style," as though the subject of style is unworthy and of no abiding value. The concept of style continues to be slighted as something that smacks of the vagaries of fashion—more whim than substance. This distaste for style, however, only makes sense if one clutches to the idea that through truth, reason, and rationality one can know of and present something of universal value. The implications of maintaining or abandoning this point of view can be clarified to some degree by examining its parallel in moral philosophy.

UNIVERSALIST AND PARTICULAR MORAL PHILOSOPHIES

Universalist moral theories provide comprehensive accounts of the moral import of an action or state of affairs. Nothing escapes the purview of God's will, or the greatest good for the greatest number, or the formula of universal law, to name the foundations of three such theories. Universalist theories that eschew God's will as a foundation derive their methods from Enlightenment confidence in the Kantian tradition of rational thought or in the utilitarian tradition of scientific method. These theories reflect a belief in the transcendent power of reason and objectivity; in the ability to identify an ultimate source of value. Particularist, or tailored, moral theories make no such claim at comprehensiveness. These outlooks—they may not even deserve to be called theories—offer piecemeal and even contradictory ideas regarding the morality of a given situation. Virtue theory is often characterized as such an outlook. Even if one is inclined to grant that the virtues are the sole legitimate basis for morality, reconciling the "excellences of character," as Aristotle called the virtues, with one another once the list becomes well-rounded is notoriously difficult.[4] Particularist theories emphasize the facts of human limitation and the patchwork of institutions and conventions out of which civilization develops. The thought that one could transcend these limitations is, according to this line of thought, a vanity.[5]

An important critique of universalist moral theories such as utilitarianism and Kantian deontic theory is that they so overrate the importance of consistency in moral judgments that they strip the otherwise conceptually rich content of morality to one concept of the good.[6] In the case of consequentialist theories such as utilitarianism, this one concept is to maximize the good in the world. For Kant, the ultimate measure was the rational being acting from his perceived duties. Critics of such monotonic conceptions of the good think that the liabilities of making all other goods instrumental toward the one good speak for themselves. They see no weakness in encouraging a more tailored outlook by foregoing a claim to universal consistency.

A related argument leveled at universalistic moralities that also applies to modernism and its progeny is that such moralities necessarily incorporate one value or one insight that is somehow ultimate, and therefore privileged and untestable. With utilitarianism, this ultimate good is something like "the greatest good for the greatest number," a good that is supposedly so self-evident that it needs no further justification; nor can one be provided without admitting that whatever justifies "the greatest good" is actually the ultimate justification. Modernists and their heirs also privilege an ultimate value. For modernists, function is sovereign; for postmodernists, the good resides in heterogeneity; for deconstructionists, the puzzling truth is that there is no ultimate truth; for neoclassicists, the ultimate truth lies in longevity.

Moral philosophy's recent reappraisal of the Aristotelian approach to morality—what is generally called virtue theory—signals the exhaustion of the universalist approach. Contemporary philosophers have thrown over the idea that a moral theory can provide consistent answers to all questions that arise in the messy human construction of morality. They think promise lies in resuscitating Aristotle's idea that morality lies in traits of character and not the relative merit or liability of any particular action. Adopting this stance is not hard if we fully accept the implications of the observation that humans are, after all, limited beings. Once we accept the fact of human limitation, it would be vainglorious to think that we could efficiently guide each decision in such a way as to account for the infinite repercussions of our actions, or that we could act as rationally as Kant demands. We humans are doomed to never have a God's-eye-view of things; given this simple observation, it seems obvious that if we desire nevertheless to behave ethically, then we should focus our work on the one thing we do, at least, have some control over—ourselves. Thus, Aristotle entreats us to develop the "excellences of character" that will enable us to act from the best self that we can be or can imagine ourselves to be.

Such an outlook no longer presumes the existence of one best action for any given situation. It presumes just the opposite. Given that you and I are limited in different ways, my action resulting from my best efforts is likely to differ from yours. This is not cause for despair, but rather, for celebration of human diversity amidst the desire for community, especially if we are able to sustain a dialogue with one another over the contents of our different points of view. Given that humans are unable to act perfectly rationally, but only in response to their strengths and weaknesses, each person develops a characteristic set of coping strategies. We would presumably all like to be perfectly kind, courageous, intelligent, athletic, prudent, interesting, and loving, but the implication of finitude is that this is not possible. Thus, one person may have long suits in courage but, of necessity, be less prudent than someone. Another may excel at getting things done, but be a tyrant as an employer. We exercise our strengths and try to overcome our weaknesses, but we simply will not be able to do everything equally well. What we do try to do is to establish a reasonably coherent outlook that matches our (limited) resources. Regarding the world from one's set of excellences and weaknesses becomes, in effect, one's style. Thus, from this perspective, to develop a personal style is not to engage in personal window dressing; it is just the best we can do.

Virtue theory cannot claim all-embracing applicability, or full explanatory value, without becoming a universalist moral theory in its own right. For virtue theory to remain on the side of a particularist outlook it must remain modest in its claims. It cannot, for example, claim to provide a final ideal of the virtuous person. Nor can it claim that reference to the virtues will be adequate armament to battle all moral dilemmas. It may turn out instead that the concept of morality is only meant to be applicable in certain situations—namely, that requiring consideration of one's position within society at large. Morality may be wholly inadequate to regulate interpersonal affairs with intimates and friends; it may be meaningless in situations where society at large has no legitimate interest. Virtue theory is unable to take a stand either for or against these possibilities without losing its particularist credentials, because to say definitively that morality does or does not apply in a given situation is to assume the God's-eye view of perfect rationality or knowledge of the ultimate good that virtue theory's proponents claim is unnecessary—a claim that is crucial for the appeal of virtue theory in the first place.

Another way to side virtue theory with the particularists, against the universalists, is to take up the criticism often leveled at Aristotle—that he is too enmeshed in a particular lifestyle to be widely applicable—and make this liability into an asset. If we agree that Aristotle had a limited outlook and audience in mind (i.e., Athenian patricians) and argue that this is all anyone can really have anyway, this criticism of virtue theory is blunted. The Aristotelian approach places great stock in the existence of conventions approved by a moral community as a precondition to acting morally. The task of morality, then, becomes not so much to construct a universal tent covering everyone as to convince others to come in under the tent they find most hospitable. This is exactly how a style operates.

A style must be sufficiently appealing and capacious for others to want to join in its conventions. Like the adherents of a given moral system, all the proponents of a given style can hope for is that the conventions they employ and the ends they hope to gain from these activities are resilient in the face of new demands, satisfying to those within the community, and compelling to others on the outside. A certain shared history, or a certain shared political outlook, is required at the outset. At bottom is an act of faith.

The idea that morality is not universally applicable is reinforced by the commonsense application it is given in architecture. Moral dilemmas regarding the public good, for example, recede in the design of private residences. Architects and owners have considerably more leeway in private residences than they do in buildings likely to receive the trusting public. The idea that moral concerns are not universally applicable makes sense of this in a way that utilitarianism cannot. For the utilitarian, even the design of private residences is an occasion for a deliberation on architecture's place in the world.

Architecture also informs and is informed by this discussion through the concept of style. Not only does the concept of style presume human limitation in means, but the existence of any given style presumes the limitation of its own applicability. A style may be marvelously supple and extensible, but it goes against the very concept to insist that any given style is infinitely, universally applicable. Architects work within a style precisely because of the absence of a privileged point of view. A tradition develops out of architects working out different answers to problems within a given mode of expression. Framing the answers to problems of expression in a communal language allows others to understand and appreciate the contributions they make to the ongoing dialogue. This helps make up for the absence of a privileged point of view. The authority of one's work, then, depends not so much on its extraordinary objectivity or prescience (much less artistic greatness or superior functioning), but rather, on its participation in this dialogue.

STYLE AND VIRTUE

The idea that one could somehow design at a level that undercuts the notion of style is reinforced by Le Corbusier's illustrations of steamships and grain silos in *Towards a New Architecture*, Sybil Moholy-Nagy's *Native Genius in Anonymous Architecture*, and Heidegger's celebrated essay "Building, Dwelling, Thinking."[7] Interest in indigenous architecture— both for its forms, in Moholy-Nagy, as well as for the manner of living it supports, as described in Heidegger—bespeaks a desire to go behind what they see as facile self-assertion that for them obscures a deeper sense of style. We should question the assumption that style obscures deeper truths. That Heidegger and others should think that arbitrary, willful design decisions would be part and parcel of working within a style, we could argue, was more a circumstance of a peculiar historic situation. This concept of style arose from a distaste for the riot of Victorian styles. It does not follow, however, that the self-conscious and the willful are necessary elements of style. Can this self-consciousness be overcome? Can an architect work within the classical tradition, for example, and have it just feel natural? The answer must be a qualified "yes." A whole generation of American classicists, for example, were working with great conviction up until World War II. Their classicism was practiced with authority and verve for over one-hundred-and-fifty years. For these architects, the conventions of classicism were much more than a means of clothing an otherwise unselfconscious structure; classicism was an expression of self.

The desire on the part of modernists to discard classical conventions may speak more to the architects' urge to cloak their identities in an anonymous rationality than to lay bare Victorian excess. Phrasing the nineteenth-century problem of style in terms of rationality proved to be highly persuasive. The charge that a work of architecture is less than rational carries with it an immediate ethical charge of its being less good than it could be. Thus, since style is highly dependent on conventions, which are not necessarily rational, the attraction of indigenous building is clear; such structures carry with them the presumption of superior rationality.

The second aspect of this bias against style—that it entails a necessary arbitrariness—is not so easily put into context. The idea of style not only depends on human limitation, but also on the existence of choice. Lacking choices, it is hard to see how an architect could be said to work within a style. The functionalist answer to the existence of choice is to do whatever maximizes the good, thereby dispelling the problem of arbitrariness.

Virtue theory offers a different answer: to act as well as one can out of the traits of character a person has at his or her disposal. One implicitly recognizes that they could act in a way other than the one they have chosen and that therefore a certain amount of individual discretion is involved. The concept of style does presume a certain arbitrariness in one's decisions. The question to put to Heidegger and Moholy-Nagy is whether their presumption that this is a bad thing is indeed justified. From the point of view of human limitation, it is hard to see how this could be a bad thing. The fact of discretion seems inevitable in the absence of perfect knowledge and perfect rationality. Both Heidegger and Moholy-Nagy want to get around this by championing a time when choices were much more restricted than they are in ours, to a time of primitive technologies and near-subsistence living when the choices were extremely limited. Thus, their presumption that arbitrariness is a bad thing is dependent on a certain revulsion at the sheer amount of choice available in modern times and nostalgia for a simpler time of very few real choices. Aversion to the superabundance of choices that seem to be the very *raison d'etre* behind the Renaissance, the Enlightenment, modern technology, and the market economy is behind the sentiment championing stylessness over style. The idea of maximizing choice, and hence approving of the fact of style, is deeply ingrained within Western culture, but so is a certain unease about it. This may be one of the tensions we have simply decided to live with, rather than reconcile. Revulsion over the excessively arbitrary and opulent acts as a brake; one yearns for simpler times and dismisses style as "mere style."

Given the role of style in creating and furthering human community, to have initiated a new style should be seen as an unparalleled cultural service. Whether it be Pablo Picasso with Cubism, Frank Lloyd Wright with the Prairie Style, or Walter Gropius with the International Style, to have assembled a coherent vocabulary of techniques, forms, and conventions so unique as to be recognizable as a new style and robust enough to encourage others to work within it, must be seen as a supremely worthwhile achievement. Cubism, the Prairie Style, and the International Style organized our perceptions in ways that were formerly inaccessible and opened up new areas of exploration for artists. This is no small feat. An outlook that denigrates such achievements as "mere style" must be off-track somewhere. Where it derails is in its incorporation of a moral outlook requiring universality.

Frank Lloyd Wright's Prairie Style opened the imagination up to ways of perceiving the world that were previously unimaginable. For this he deserves high praise. That he would dismiss others practicing in the Prairie Style as inferior imitators only shows how little regard he had for his own achievement. To say of postmodernism or of deconstruction that it constituted a style is to pay a high compliment. To charge that it never achieved the status of becoming a recognizable style would be the criticism. Postmodernism allowed architects to make statements through their art that modernism never allowed. What never quite happened, unhappily, was that it never became a full-fledged style, in the sense of establishing a tradition of recognizable conventions and motifs that practitioners could explore, embellish, and purify. Rather, postmodernism always wanted to be a critique, an avant-garde movement. Once its avant-gardism was spent, the movement was spent too. The same sentiments characterized deconstruction, and the same criticism applies.

To have created a new style of architecture does nothing less than provide new ways of seeing, new means of expression, new ways of coping with the world, and not least importantly, new ways of reinventing community by creating new dialogues. To work within a style is to enjoy the community of one's peers and to capitalize on the work of one's precursors. To have created a style is to have given a gift to the world, an ethical achievement of high order.

THE VIRTUOUS BUILDING

How does this lionizing of style square with David Watkin's formidable critique of theorists such as A. W. N. Pugin, Eugene-Emmanuel Viollet-le-duc and Sir Nicholas Pevsner, who justified stylistic preferences on moral grounds?[8] This argument cannot but agree with Watkin's, that seeking to justify a given style by asserting its moral superiority is a doomed enterprise. To do so is to invoke the privileged point of view that does not exist. We may find that a given style is instrumentally better than another for our purposes, but this need not lead to the erroneous conclusion of Watkin's targets that their preferred styles were ultimately, objectively, or morally better. The moral question in relation to style then, is not over which one is morally superior, but rather the ends each one is fashioned to serve. Once again, Watkin's admonition to avoid moralizing style does not hold true against just any type of moral theory. The types of moral outlooks Pugin, Viollet-le-duc and Pevsner were seeking to justify their stylistic preferences against were universalistic theories of action; theories that claim to apply to all rational beings or all moral agents. By sticking to arguments championing certain social evils, Pugin and his successors might have fared better, but then they would have had to construct a case for the inevitability of their favored style given those ends. It is doubtful, however, that such inevitability can be demonstrated.

If one considers morality to be solely about best actions or proper intentions, then of course it makes sense to dispute whether, from a moral standpoint, it makes any difference if bricks are stacked into a pointed arch or a round arch. These various arrangements of bricks are good or bad only to the extent they facilitate good or bad results or reflect good or bad intentions. Short of stacking them so that they fall over and kill someone, it is silly to claim that my stack is more moral than yours. To impart moral worth to inanimate objects—objects that have neither intentions nor actions— is nonsensical. Doing so leads to exactly the sort of instrumentalism Hannah Arendt criticized so forcefully, in which things we would like to value in their own right are valued only for what they contribute to a utilitarian conception of the good. If, however, one looks to particular arrangements of bricks for what they further or hinder in the way of community dialogue or artistic traditions, or what they reflect of community values, then these arrangements of inanimate objects no longer appear quite so morally neutral. Given this outlook, sentiments against Stalinist neoclassicism and antebellum Greek Revival architecture need not be dismissed as emotional hangovers directed at morally reprehensible regimes. The buildings that make up these stylistic moments were part and parcel of the power structure on which these oppressive cultures were based. These styles facilitated their builders and owners' participation in certain cultural conversations—about domination, racism, totalitarianism— that we find reprehensible. One need not subscribe to the idea that these structures possess latent properties that made them morally inferior to recognize that the choices made in these arrangements of bricks were not entirely arbitrary and that it serves future generations to become familiar with their motifs. If a style can be expressive of virtue, it can be equally expressive of vice.

Contemporary insistence on universality has charged criticism with forever disputing the ground rules in an endless game of one-upmanship, and the cause of architecture is much the worse for it. Self-consciousness has replaced perceptiveness; theory has replaced criticism; provenance has replaced tradition. Architects need not go back to the Middle Ages to rediscover a time when artists worked knowingly within a style and with unabashed connoisseurship. They do, perhaps, need to go back as far as the eighteenth century, before the Victorian era so cheapened the concept of style that it could no longer be trusted. Contemporary mistrust of stylistic conventions makes unattainable the daring incisiveness of a Denis Diderot, who understood the art and artists of the Paris Salons of the 1750s so intimately that he could, say, extract the character of artist Jean-Baptiste Greuze from one of his paintings:

> He's a bit vain, our painter, but his vanity is that of a child, it's the intoxication of talent. Deprive him of the naiveté that enables him to say of his own work: Look at that, how beautiful it is! . . . and you'll deprive him of verve, you'll extinguish his fire, and his genius will be eclipsed. I suspect that if he were to become modest he'd have no further reason for being. Our best qualities are closely related to our faults.[9]

Diderot's extraordinarily lively comments were made possible by the reassuring presumption of a community of knowledgeable, perceptive, and like-minded readers. Such comments made today would turn Diderot's presumption into presumptuousness. The demand for universal value discourages personality, and architecture is no longer allowed the faults of its virtues. By regarding style to be an inevitable expression of self, and the self to be not an isolated individual but a participant in community struggle, architects stand to rehabilitate the subject of style as a fitting subject of serious discussion. A vibrant style with which to give form to the values and dilemmas of our culture is the missing element needed for an architecture of unparalleled relevance.

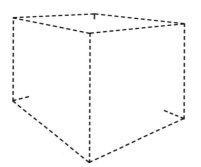

EPILOGUE

Serious discussion about the ethical dilemmas of architectural design has existed on the margins of architectural discourse, largely because it has not been especially fruitful. At fault is the piecemeal treatment that the subject has received, wherein the basic values of architectural design are considered apart from an architect's professional ethics. Architects, in practice, cannot—and in discussion, should not—separate the two. By considering the architect's ethical milieu as one in which the desires to be both a conscientious professional and a good designer are inextricably conjoined, the full bite of the problem emerges. This does not mean that easy solutions to design dilemmas will automatically present themselves, but it does help to focus the discussion and to eliminate a few impediments enabling morality to become a more integral part of architectural discourse.

One of those impediments is the tendency for the discussion to lapse into endless regressions. The temptation to recontextualize a design dilemma as a symptom of a larger or more abstract problem is strong, especially in situations in which an architect encounters unexpected difficulties in balancing competing demands on scant resources. Does the program need to be rewritten? Is the design serving the wrong masters? Is the architect overstepping his or her bounds by making a certain decision? Do the social, economic, and professional contexts need to be rethought before responsible design decisions can be made? The prospect of regress is so daunting that it tempts some architects to turn their backs on the discussion altogether, thus relegating the ethical dimension of architecture to the responsibility of others: sociologists, social-rights activists, politicians and policy-makers. The repudiation of architecture's valiant effort to unify the artistic and the ethical within the modern movement only reinforces this temptation.

A contractarian outlook reins in the problem of regress. Architects may call a halt to the process of recontextualization, get on with designing for the problem at hand, and be confident they are doing so with the uncoerced consent of society by cleaving to a mutually beneficial contract, sealed with the architect's registration stamp. By accepting the idea of the professional practice of architecture as the locus for a certain bundle of societal dilemmas concerned with the built environment, practice is sufficiently well-defined for design deliberations to proceed, but not so constrained as to cause the ethical import of design decisions to wither away. The upshot is that architects can expect to experience a certain unease about their decisions, but this unease is not necessarily a bad thing. This is the role an architect in this society has accepted, and it is actually a fine role to perform. Architects have every right and obligation to jealously guard against those who would denigrate the importance of this role by assuming its benefits without taking on its responsibilities.

Another impediment to ethics joining the mainstream of architectural discourse has been the idea that design deliberations ultimately solve dilemmas irrationally unless the architect privileges a single, ultimate value—something taken to be "good in all cases" Utility is usually held to be that

206

ultimate arbiter. Not only does utility fail to provide an adequate account of architecture's basic values, however, but in the absence of constraints it is also subject to regress. This concept of design rationality solves the dilemmas of design all too quickly and forces an unrealistic unity of aims on the process of resolving the disparate demands that play into design. Sensing this, architects have been right to avoid such discussion. Rejecting an ultimate measure for design merit or moral worth implies a plurality of values—and a fresh set of moral problems.

One problem often perceived to follow from plural conceptions of value is that such views lead inexorably to a pernicious relativism—that no uncoercive basis can be established for preferring one design solution over another. The longevity and stability of the Vitruvian conception of architecture's basic values, however, would argue in favor of exactly the opposite conclusion. Not only do the values of *firmitas*, *utilitas*, and *venustas* survive close scrutiny, they provide some benchmarks for evaluating other claims to the title of "basic architectural value."

The prospect of acknowledging a plurality of design values has also been shied away from in the past because it offers no systematic means for resolving conflict. Lack of consistency, however, proves a lesser peril than the requirement of systematic methods to discard important sources for informing design thinking. The moral complexity implied in a plurality of values is one of the things that makes design a source of fascination and allows it to be such a marvelously supple contributor to contemporary life. By rejecting design models that postulate universal measures of value, architects have traded in a brittle reliability for durability and relevance—a good trade, but one that requires a thorough and ongoing defense of those values we take to be irreducible. This defense

207

must be mounted anew every day as the products of architects' design thinking are given over to public scrutiny.

Systematic and utilitarian design theories lionize a portrayal of the designer as an anonymous, detached, scientifically rational diagnostician. The ethical discussion is only further eroded by this image, however, because it leaves behind the strong impression that the dilemmas must be resolved through improved methods and diagnostic techniques. Some may prefer this model, as it allows the architect a certain amount of refuge behind the apparent detachment and anonymity. A more full-blooded portrayal places a much greater burden on the architect as a human being, with all the characteristic strengths, weaknesses, limitations, and moments of transcendence this implies. This portrayal stands to enrich the discussion immeasurably by making design out to be fundamentally informed by the dilemmas of the human condition not just in its consequences, but throughout. By distancing ourselves from the model of impersonal rationality, the ability to design becomes more closely aligned with personal development than with mechanical skill.

This personal development cannot be undertaken as successfully in isolation as it can in dialogue with fellow inquirers. Any means we have to strengthen this dialogue are worth pursuing. Certainly, the logical place to start is to encourage as rich and as inclusive a community discussion as possible. Architects are fortunate that they have at their disposal not only a tradition of verbal discourse, but also one of conversing through the objects of their making, lodged within the built environment—a source that often provides the most eloquent arguments of all. A well-crafted, thoroughly argued design ethic can add to this dialogue, thereby serving to help architects develop their vision in an admittedly contentious, but otherwise receptive, world.

NOTES

BIBLIOGRAPHY

INDEX

1. "Air Terminal Turns Leaky," *Rome News Tribune,* 15 September 1991. "Woes Mount for Terminal Designer," *Rome News Tribune,* 17 September 1991. "Terminal Designer [   ] Says Building's Problem 'Not Major,'" *Rome News Tribune*, 19 September 1991. "Terminal Totally Defective," *Rome News Tribune*, 20 September 1991. "Airport Repairs On Hold Until Commission Receives Reports," *Rome News Tribune*, 27 September 1991. "[   ] Charged for Practicing Without License," *Rome News Tribune*, 3 October 1991. "Airport Architect Enters Guilty Plea," *Rome News Tribune*, 26 May 1992.

2. "Doss: [   ] Should Foot Terminal Repair Bill," *Rome News Tribune,* 27 May 1992.

3. *The Law Governing Practice of Architecture in Georgia*, sec. 43-4-14, states, "the board shall have power to suspend or revoke the certificate of registration" for, among other things, the "conviction by any court of record of the United States of any act which would constitute a felony or a crime involving moral turpitude in this state or a plea of *nolo contendere* to any such charge." California is a bit more vague on this matter:

   > For the purposes of denial, suspension, or revocation of the license of an architect pursuant to Division 1.5 (commencing with Section 475) of the Business and Professions Code, a crime of act shall be considered substantially related to the qualifications, functions and duties of an architect if to a substantial degree it evidences present or potential unfitness of an architect to perform the functions authorized by his/her license in a manner consistent with the public health, safety or welfare. Such crimes or acts shall include, but not be limited to, those involving the following: (a) Any violation of the provisions of Chapter 3 Division 3 of the Business and Professions Code.

   California Board of Architectural Examiners, *The Architects Practice Act* (Sacramento, 1996), sec. 110.

4. B. Barber, "Some Problems in the Sociology of the Professions," *Daedalus* 92 (1963): 669. Dana Cuff, "The Architecture Profession," in *The Architect's Handbook of Professional Practice*, ed. David Haviland (Washington, D.C.: American Institute of Architects, 1988), part 1.2, 2–4. Andy Pressman, *Professional Practice 101* (New York: John Wiley & Sons, 1997). Carl Sapers, "Practice: Should Interior Designers be Licensed?" *Architectural Record* 6 (June 1988): 37–47.
5. Bernard Williams, "Professional Morality and Its Dispositions," in *Making Sense of Humanity and Other Philosophical Papers, 1982–1993* (Cambridge, UK: Cambridge University Press, 1995), 196.
6. Henry Cobb, "Ethics and Architecture," *Harvard Architecture Review* 8, no. 44 (1992): 47–48.
7. Thomas Hobbes, *The Leviathan* (1651) (Amherst, NY: Prometheus Books, 1988), 69.
8. See John Rawls, *A Theory of Justice* (Cambridge, MA: Harvard University Press, 1971), and David Gauthier, *Morals by Agreement* (Oxford: Clarendon Press, 1986).
9. Rawls, *A Theory of Justice*, 4.13, and Gauthier, *Morals by Agreement*, 10.
10. The making and fulfilling of promises between architects and clients and architects and society is the genesis of the moral content of professional practice.
11. Magali Larson, *The Rise of Professionalism* (Berkeley: University of California Press, 1977).
12. For conflict theory, see Robert W. Clarke and Robert P. Lawry, *The Power of the Professional Person* (New York: University Press of America, 1988) and John Kultgen, *Ethics and Professionalism* (Philadelphia: University of Pennsylvania Press, 1988).

13. Larson does not deny that architecture deals with matters of moral import, but she does take a view in *The Rise of Professionalism* that is dubious of the concept of "professional morality." Elsewhere, she states, "I submit that asking what kind of architectural objects should be built, in what kind of cities, and for whose comfort and delight, are crucial (if not the most crucial) *theoretical* questions architects can ask for themselves." In William S. Saunders, ed., *Reflections on Architectural Practices in the Nineties* (New York: Princeton Architectural Press, 1996), 141.
14. Dana Cuff, *Architecture: The Story of Practice* (Cambridge, MA: MIT Press, 1991), especially 68–69.
15. David Brain, "Practical Knowledge and Occupational Control—The Professionalization of Architecture in the United States," *Sociological Forum* (June 1991): 240.
16. Bruce A. Kimball, *The Professionalization of America: The Emergence of the "True Professional Ideal"* (Cambridge, UK: Blackwell, 1992).
17. See, for instance, Moshe Safdie, "Architecture in Search of an Ethic," *The Canadian Architect* (November 1991): 44, and Cobb, "Ethics and Architecture."
18. Christopher Alexander, "Perspectives: Manifesto 1991," *Progressive Architecture* (July 1991): 108–12.
19. Alexander, "Manifesto."
20. Alexander, "Manifesto," 112.
21. The American Institute of Architects, *Standard Form of Agreement Between Owner and Architect, Document B141*, secs. 2.4.15 and 2.4.16, states:
    > The Architect shall interpret and decide matters concerning performance of the Owner and Contractor under the requirements of the Contract Documents on written request of either the Owner or Contractor. . . . Interpretations and decisions of the Architect shall be consistent with the intent of and reasonably inferable from the Contract Documents and shall be in writing or in the form of drawings. When making such interpretations and initial decisions, the Architect shall endeavor to secure faithful performance by both Owner and Contractor, shall not show partiality to either, and shall not be liable for results of interpretations or decisions so rendered in good faith.
22. Jerrold Sonet, "Practice: Should Interior Designers be Licensed?" *Architectural Record* 6 (June 1988), 37.
23. Sonet, "Practice: Should Interior Designers be Licensed," 37.
24. "International Code Council & The Model Descriptive Building Codes: What's Happening and What's Next?" www.asid.org/ethics/codeqa.htm., 9 February 2000.

212

As one interior designer put it, "It is basically a matter of protection of and the preservation of our rights to practice as design professionals." Cited in Sonja Roberts and Tom Baldwin, "Practice: Title Registration for Interior Designers," *Iowa Architect* 40, no. 2 (Summer 1991): 40–41. This puts the interior designer in the role of the beleaguered one, only trying to protect him or herself and ignoring the obvious question, "Who said you were a design professional in the first place?"

The ASID code of ethics states, "Members shall at all times consider the health, safety and welfare of the public in spaces they design. Members agree, whenever possible, to notify property managers, landlords, and/or public officials of conditions within a built environment that endanger the health, safety and/or welfare of occupants." ASID, *Code of Ethics and Professional Conduct* (www.asid.org/ethics/member_coe.htm), sec. 2.3.

25. Although this effort was successful with changing the language in the International Building Code, it remains to be seen whether the individual states will go along. In states that have enacted interior design practice legislation, it is assumed that the code, when adopted, will allow interior designers to stamp drawings for the purpose of permits.

1. Vitruvius, *The Ten Books on Architecture*, trans. Morris Hickey Morgan (New York: Dover Publications, 1960), Book I, Chapter III, Section 2.

    Since about 30–20 BCE, when Vitruvius wrote the *Ten Books on Architecture*, the text has been translated into countless languages. English translations have varied widely in their interpretation of the terms *firmitas*, *utilitas*, and *venustas*. In his 1624 edition, Henry Wotton translated the terms as "firmness," "commodity," and "delight," while Rowland and Howe selected "soundness," "utility," and "attractiveness" for use in their 1999 volume, thus amending the Morgan translation, first published in 1914, of "durability, convenience, and beauty." Like the English, Italian translations have varied over time, from "solidità," "utilità," and "venustà," in the earliest versions to *"fermezza," "comodo,"* and *"bellézza"* in the 1978 Florian translation. French translations have been more consistent: The 1816 Boil, 1909 Choisy, and 1990 Fleury translations all give the terms as *"solidité," "utilité,"* and *"beauté."* By employing the Latin terms in this discussion, the author hopes to allow the normative potential of these words to emerge in the course of the discussion.

2. Vitruvius, *Ten Books*, Book I, Ch. I, sec. 7. In the introduction to Book VI, sec. 6, Vitruvius discusses the value of an architect as a "good man," or man of honor.

3. Robert Venturi, *Complexity and Contradiction in Architecture* (New York: Museum of Modern Art, 1977), 16.

4. Charles Jencks, "Death for Rebirth," in *Post-Modernism on Trial*, ed. Andreas Papadakis (London: Academy Editions, 1990), 6.

5. Leon Battista Alberti, *On the Art of Building in Ten Books*, trans. Joseph Rykwert (Cambridge, MA: MIT Press, 1996). Alberti asserts, "Of the three conditions that apply to every form of construction—that what we construct should be appropriate to its use, lasting in structure, and graceful and pleasing in appearance." Alberti, *On the Art of Building*, 155.

   Alberti's views were considerably more psychologically subtle than those of Vitruvius. Alberti subscribed both to the Aristotelian conception of the virtues and to the need to exercise them in their proper amounts (neither too little nor too much). He wrote, "For to build is a matter of necessity; to build conveniently is the product both of necessity and utility; but to build something praised by the magnificent, yet not rejected by the frugal, is the province only of an artist of experience, wisdom, and thorough deliberation." Alberti, *On the Art of Building*, 315. Alberti also held the Platonic conception that a perfected, or ideal, architecture was the fitting aim of the architect.

6. Henry Wotton, *The Elements of Architecture* (1624, reprinted Farnborough: Gregg International Publishers Ltd., 1969).

7. Sir William Chambers, *A Treatise on the Decorative Part of Civil Architecture* (1791, reprinted New York: Benjamin Blom, 1968), B.

8. Cited in Goerd Peschken, *Das Architektonische Lehrbuch (Karl Friedrich Schinkel, Lebenswerk)* (Munich: 1979), cited in Hanno-Walter Kruft, *A History of Architectural Theory from Vitruvius to the Present* (New York: Princeton Architectural Press, 1994), 299.

9. These ideas derive from Samuel Scheffler's notion of the tensions between liberalism and particularism, presented in "Liberalism, Associative Duties, and the Boundaries of Responsibility," unpublished paper, delivered at the 1994–5 John Dewey Memorial Lecture, University of Vermont.

   Proponents of postmodernism might counter that the theory did show the existence of commonalities beyond a mere desire for plurality: a rediscovered interest in history; an embrace of kitschy popular culture; a friendlier version of monumentality than modernism was able to summon; and, most importantly, a new appreciation for the diversity inherent in urban life. These are valid objections, but the question remains, what are the social pretensions of postmodernism, as opposed to its salutary by-products, and has it left us any basis for disagreement?

10. David Watkin, *Morality and Architecture* (Oxford: Clarendon Press, 1977), 38.

11. Venturi, *Complexity and Contradiction*, 16.

12. Venturi, *Complexity and Contradiction*, 41.

13. Venturi, *Complexity and Contradiction*, 18.
14. "When circumstances defy order, order should bend or break: anomalies and uncertainties give validity to architecture." Venturi, *Complexity and Contradiction*, 41.
15. Alberti, *On the Art of Building in Ten Books*, Book Six, sec. 2, 156.
16. Watkin, in particular, covers this territory well with regard to moral argument. See his *Morality and Architecture* (Oxford: Clarendon Press, 1977), esp. chapters 1 and 2.
17. Jean-François Lyotard labels "a distrust of metanarratives" the hallmark of a postmodern outlook. See his *The Postmodern Condition: A Report on Knowle*dge (Minneapolis: University of Minnesota Press, 1984), xxiv–xxv.
18. See Karsten Harries, *The Ethical Function of Architecture* (Cambridge, MA: MIT Press, 1997), 25.
19. Harries, *The Ethical Function of Architecture*, 25.
20. See Martin Heidegger, "Building, Dwelling, Thinking," in *Poetry, Language, Thought* (New York: Harper & Row, 1971).
21. Heidegger presumably would answer this objection by arguing that the demand for objective verification is part of the initial problem. Without some insistence on a neutral ground, however, nothing stands in the way of utter subjectivity and the resulting inability to address issues of communal concern. These potential objections aside, a return to the elemental in architecture may well provide a rich avenue for exploration.
22. In the *Republic*, Plato states, "ugliness and discord and inharmonious motion are nearly allied to ill words and ill nature, as grace and harmony are the twin sisters of goodness and self-restraint and bear their likeness." Trans. Henry Desmond Pritchard Lee (Baltimore: Penguin, 1974), 401. To make this connection, Plato realizes he must distinguish between the base motive of pleasure and the higher motive of the "good." He does so in *Gorgias*, trans. T. Irwin (Oxford: Clarendon Press, 1929), 501, in which he discusses how good does not aim at pleasure. Without this guidance, "vice and intemperance and meanness and deformity in sculpture and building and the other creative arts" would arise and "silently gather a festering mass of corruption in their own soul." Better to let the true artists guide, Plato advises, "then will our youth dwell in a land of health, amid fair sights and sounds, and receive the good in everything; and beauty, the effluence of fair works, shall flow into the eye and ear, like a health-giving breeze from a purer region, insensibly draw the soul from earliest years into likeness and sympathy with the beauty of reason." *Republic*, 401.
23. Ludwig Wittgenstein, *Tractatus Logico-Philosophicus*, trans. D. F. Pears and B. F. McGuinness (1921, reprinted London: Routledge and Kegun Paul,

215

1961), prop. 6.421, 71. Paul Wijdeveld, *Ludwig Wittgenstein, Architect* (Cambridge, MA: MIT Press, 1994), 184.

24. G. E. Moore, *Principia Ethica* (Buffalo, NY: Prometheus Books, 1988), 201. In 1927, DeWitt Parker wrote, "As Plato devined, the form of the good and the form of the beautiful are the same." "Wish Fulfillment and Imagination," in *Proceedings of the Sixth International Congress of Philosophy* (1927), 439.

25. Ernest Gombrich, *Meditations on a Hobby Horse* (London: Phaidon Press, 1985), 17.

26. Eugene Emmanuel Viollet-le-duc, *The Lectures on Architecture* (1875), trans. Benjamin Bucknall (New York: Grove Press, 1959).

27. Abbé Marc-Antoine Laugier, *An Essay on Architecture* (1756), trans. Wolfgang and Anni Herrmann (Los Angeles: Hennessey & Ingalls, 1977), 11–15.

28. "Superior" is used here in the sense of "above" or "prior to," not "better than."

29. Paul Tillich, *On Art and Architecture* (New York: Crossroad Publishing Co., 1987), 26.

30. Clive Bell, "The Aesthetic Hypothesis," in *Aesthetics*, ed. Susan Feagin and Patrick Maynard (New York: Oxford University Press, 1997), 15–23.

31. José Ortega y Gasset, "An Essay in Esthetics," in *Phenomenology and Art*, trans. Philip W. Silver (New York: W. W. Norton & Co., 1975), 129.

32. R. G. Collingwood, *Principles of Art* (New York: Oxford University Press, 1938), 274; E. H. Gombrich, "Four Theories of Artistic Expression," in *Gombrich on Art and Psychology*, ed. Richard Woodfield (Manchester: Manchester University Press, 1996); Herbert Read, *Art and Society*, 2nd ed. (London: Faber & Faber, 1945), 6.

33. Marcia Muelder Eaton, "Aesthetics: The Mother of Ethics?" *The Journal of Aesthetics and Art Criticism* 55, no. 4 (Fall 1997): 361.

34. Eaton, "Aesthetics," 361.

35. Eaton, "Aesthetics," 361.

36. Eaton, "Aesthetics," 362.

37. Peter Eisenman and Leon Krier, "Peter Eisenman versus Leon Krier: 'My ideology is better than yours,'" *Architectural Design* 59, no. 9–10 (September/October 1989), 7.

38. Jorge Silvetti, "The Beauty of Shadows," *Oppositions* 9 (Summer 1977), 273.

39. 'Humanism' has become one of those words that means many things to many people. It is used here in Erwin Panofsky's sense, of a "conviction of the dignity of man, based on the insistence on human values (rationality and freedom) and the acceptance of human limitation." *Meaning in the Visual Arts* (Chicago: University of Chicago Press, 1982), 2.

40. The oscillation between form and function are looked upon by Silvetti, Eisenman, Anthony Vidler, and Aldo Rossi as a "game of opposites." The word "game" is used as a metaphor for the antagonism between form and function, and its use is deliberately deflating. It seeks to minimize what's at stake—to treat the antagonism in Orwellian terms, in which a "war" is reduced to a "game" by the powers that be for the purpose of subjugation.

41. Geoffrey Scott, *The Architecture of Humanism* (London: Constable and Company, 1924), 144.

42. Scott, *Architecture of Humanism*, 199.

43. Scott, *Architecture of Humanism*, 15.

44. Peter Eisenman, "Post-Functionalism," *Oppositions* 6 (Fall 1976), reprinted in *Architecture Theory Since 1968,* ed. K. Michael Hays (Cambridge, MA: MIT Press, 1998), 239.

45. Eisenman, "Post-Functionalism," 239.

46. Mary McLeod, "Architecture and Politics in the Reagan Era: From Postmodernism to Deconstructivism," *Assemblage* 8 (February 1989), reprinted in *Architecture Theory Since 1968*, 694.

47. Bernard Tschumi, "The Pleasure of Architecture," *Architectural Design* 3 (March 1977): 218.

48. McLeod, "Architecture and Politics," 697.

49. Richard Rorty, "Habermas and Lyotard on Postmodernity," in *Habermas and Modernity*, ed. Richard J. Bernstein (Cambridge, UK: Polity Press, 1985), 176.

50. Scott, *Architecture of Humanism*, 158. Italics are Scott's own.

51. Watkin, *Morality and Architecture*, 23.

52. For a critique of the problem of everything being reduced to function, see Jane Jacobs, *The Death and Life of Great American Cities* (New York: Random House, 1961). For his a humorous indictment of the tendency to torture function into some sort of artistic form, see Peter Blake, *Form Follows Fiasco: Why Modern Architecture Hasn't Worked* (Boston: Little, Brown & Co., 1977).

CHAPTER 3

1. John Stuart Mill would have us accept that some sort of standard is a requirement of any organized moral outlook. He charged that even for intuitionists and *a priorists*, "there ought either to be some one fundamental principle of law, at the root of all morality, or if there be several, there should be a determinate order of precedence among them; and the one principle, or the rule for deciding between the various principles when they conflict, ought to be self-evident." "Utilitarianism" (1861), in *Utilitarianism and Other Essays* (Oxford: Penguin Books, 1987), 274.

2. Vitruvius, *The Ten Books on Architecture* (New York: Dover Publications, 1960), Ch. III, sec. 2, 17.

3. City and County of San Francisco,"Presidio Land Use, Proposition L," *Voter Information Pamphlet, Consolidated Primary Election* (2 June 1998), 163.

4. "San Francisco's *Prop. L.*," *Forum*, KQED-FM, 19 May1998.

5. *San Francisco Voter Information Pamphlet*, 163–173

6. Introduction to *Consequentialism and its Critics*, ed. Samuel Scheffler (New York: Oxford University Press, 1988), 1.

7. The National Park Service actually conducted a cost-benefit analysis on several schemes at the Presidio. These are detailed in the United States Department of the Interior, National Park Service, *Final General Management Plan Amendment Environmental Impact Statement: Presidio of San Francisco Golden Gate National Recreation Area California* (Denver, July 1994), Appendix I, II.

8. This opinion has a distinguished philosophical pedigree, beginning with Jeremy Bentham. Bentham wrote, "By the principle of utility is meant that principle which approves or disapproves of every action whatsoever, according to the tendency which it appears to have to augment or diminish the happiness of the party whose interest is in question." *An Introduction to the Principles of Morals and Legislation* (1824), reprinted in *Utilitarianism and Other Essays*, 65. Mill restated Bentham's sentiments when he wrote, "Utility, or the Greatest Happiness Principle, holds that actions are right in proportion as they tend to promote happiness, wrong as they tend to produce the reverse of happiness." "Utilitarianism," (1861), reprinted in *Utilitarianism and Other Essays*, 279.

9. R. M. Hare, "Rights, Utility, and Universalization" in *Utility and Rights*, ed. R. G. Frey (Minneapolis: University of Minnesota Press, 1984).

10. Frederick Schick, "Under Which Descriptions?" in *Utility and Rights*, 251.

11. R. M. Hare, "Ethical Theory and Utilitarianism," in *Utilitarianism and Beyond*, ed. Amartya Sen and Bernard Williams (Cambridge, UK: Cambridge University Press, 1982), 28.

12. For a discussion of the notion that an architect's professional values are slightly at variance with those of society, see Chapter One.

13. He argues, "what the principle of utility requires of me is to do for each man affected by my actions what I wish were done for me in the hypothetical circumstances that I were in precisely his situation." Hare, "Ethical Theory and Utilitarianism," *Utilitarianism and Beyond*, 28.

14. John Harsanyi, "Morality and the Theory of Rational Behavior," in *Utilitarianism and Beyond*, 61.

15. Introduction to *Incommensurability, Incomparability, and Practical Reason*, ed. Ruth Chang (Cambridge, MA: Harvard University Press, 1997), 5.

16. Conversation with Cary Fierobend, a planner with the National Park Service assigned to the Presidio, San Francisco,18 March 1998.

17. Steven Lukes, "Comparing the Incomparable: Trade-Offs and Sacrifices," in *Incommensurability, Incomparability, and Practical Reason*, 188.

18. Bernard Williams noted this tendency towards regress when he wrote, "No one can hold that everything, of whatever category, that has value, has it in virtue of its consequences. If that were so, one would just go on for ever, and there would be an obviously hopeless regress." Bernard Williams, *Utilitarianism: For and Against* (Cambridge, UK: Cambridge University Press, 1973), 82.

19. See, for instance, R. A. Moshini, "On Measuring Project Performance: Some Problems of Aggregation," in *Evaluating and Predicting Design Performance,* ed. Yehuda Kalay (New York: John Wiley & Sons, 1992), 246–47; Avi Weizel and Rachel Becker, "Integration of Performance Evaluation in Computer-Aided Design," *Evaluating and Predicting Design Performance* (New York: John Wiley & Sons, 1992), 173; G. S. Shabha, "Development of Objective Methods for Measuring Flexibility of School Buildings," in *Design and Decision Support Systems in Architecture*, ed. Harry Timmermans (Boston: Kluwer Academic Publishers, 1993), 172.

20. Introduction to *Incommensurability, Incomparability, and Practical Reason*, 18.

21. For instance, Stuart Hampshire wrote, "Individuals inevitably become conscious of the cost exacted by their own way of life and of the other possibilities of achievement and enjoyment discarded. They feel the cost in internal conflict also. Every established way of life has its cost in repression." *Morality and Conflict* (Cambridge, MA: Harvard University Press, 1983), 147. Alasdair MacIntyre wrote, "morality is always to some degree tied to the socially local and particular and that the aspirations of the morality of modernity to a universality freed from all particularity is an illusion . . . that there is no way to possess the virtues except as part of a tradition in which we inherit them and our understanding of them from a

219

series of predecessors." *After Virtue* (South Bend, Ind.: University of Notre Dame Press, 1984), 126.

22. John Dewey, for instance, wrote, "Science is an affair of civilization not of individual intellect. So with conscience. When a child acts, those about him re-act. They shower encouragement upon him, visit him with approval, or they bestow frowns and rebuke. . . . The social environment may be as artificial as you please. But its action in response to ours is natural not artificial . . . that moral judgment and moral responsibility are the work wrought in us by the social environment, signify that all morality is social; not because we ought to take into account the effects of our acts upon the welfare of others, but because of facts." *Human Nature and Conduct*, *The Moral Writings of John Dewey,* ed. James Gouinlock (Amherst, NY: Prometheus Books, 1994), 182–83.

23. Isaiah Berlin, *Concepts and Categories* (London: Hogarth Press, 1978). See also Bernard Williams, "Conflicts of Values," in *Moral Luck* (Cambridge, UK: Cambridge University Press, 1981), 71.

24. See especially, Elizabeth Anderson, *Value in Ethics and Economics* (Cambridge, MA: Harvard University Press, 1993), 5.

25. Norman Dahl, "Morality, Moral Dilemmas and Moral Requirements," in *Moral Dilemmas and Moral Theory*, ed. H. E. Mason (Oxford: Oxford University Press, 1996), 86–101.

26. Joseph Raz, *Morality of Freedom* (Oxford: Clarendon Press, 1986), 334.

27. Joseph Raz, "Incommensurability and Agency," in *Incommensurability, Incomparability, and Practical Reason*, 125.

28. Raz, "Incommensurabilty and Agency," 128.

29. Elizabeth Anderson, *Value in Ethics and Economics*, 6.

30. Introduction, *Utilitarianism and Beyond*, 17.

1. Lewis Mumford, "The Case Against Modern Architecture," *The Lewis Mumford Reader*, ed. Donald L. Miller (New York: Pantheon Books, 1986), 77.

2. For the creation and consumption of aesthetics as communication, see R. G. Collingwood, *The Principles of Art* (New York: Oxford University Press, 1938). Others who have maintained a communication theory include Curt Ducasse, *The Philosophy of Art* (1929, reprinted New York: Dover Publications, 1966); José Ortega y Gasset, "An Essay in Esthetics by Way of a Preface," in *Phenomenology and Art,* trans. Philip W. Silver (New York: W. W. Norton & Company, 1975) and Herbert Read, *Art and Society*, 2d ed. (London: Faber and Faber, 1945).

For art as therapy, see Adrian Stokes, *The Invitation in Art* (London: Tavistock Publications, 1965). Stokes wrote, "I feel that all art describes processes by which we find ourselves to some extent carried away, and that our identification with them will have been essential to the subsequent contemplation of the work of art as an image not only of an independent and completed object but of the ego's integration." *The Invitation in Art*, 19.

For art as expression, see Benedetto Croce, *Guide to Aesthetics* (1913, reprinted Indianapolis: Hackett Publishing Co., 1965).

For art as hedonism, see George Santayana, "The Nature of Beauty," *Art and Philosophy: Readings in Aesthetics*, ed. W. E. Kennick (New York: St. Martin's Press, 1964). Santayana writes that the distinction between pleasure and the sense of beauty is "one of intensity and delicacy, not of nature." Santayana, "The Nature of Beauty," 515.

For art as cognition, see Paul Tillich, *On Art and Architecture* (New York: Crossroad Publishing Co. 1987).

For art and aesthetic perception as a form of knowledge, see Immanuel Kant, *The Critique of Judgment*, trans. James Creed Merideth (Oxford: Clarendon Press, 1952).

For the aesthetic as a necessary ingredient to a moral outlook, see E. H. Gombrich, "Four Theories of Artistic Expression," in *Gombrich on Art and Psychology,* ed. Richard Woodfield (Manchester: Manchester University Press, 1996), and E. H. Gombrich, *Meditations on a Hobby Horse and Other Essays on the Theory of Art*, 4th ed. (London: Phaidon Press, 1984). See also Marcia Muelder Eaton, "Aesthetics: The Mother of Ethics?" *The Journal of Aesthetics and Art Criticism* 55, no. 4 (Fall 1997): 355–64, and Alan H. Goldman, *Aesthetic Value (*Boulder, CO: Westview Press, 1995), 8.

For art as the backbone of cultural development, see Clement Greenberg, *Art and Culture: Critical Essays* (Boston: Beacon Press, 1961).

3. Richard Miller, "Three Versions of Objectivity," in *Aesthetics and Ethics: Essays at the Intersection*, ed. Jerrold Levinson (New York: Cambridge University Press, 1998), 51. Others do not agree with this incomparability thesis from the outset. For example, in his excellent survey of twentieth-century architectural criticism, Larry Ligo argued that "in most cases in which a critic praises a building for its artistic value in spite of practical failings, what he senses about the building—though he often does not verbalize it—is that is 'functions' well on the cultural/existential level." Larry L. Ligo, *The Concept of Function in Twentieth-Century Architectural Criticism* (1974, reprinted Ann Arbor: UMI Research Press, 1984), 79–80. He showed that cultural/existential criticism is on the rise, especially since 1950 and thought that this criticism "encompasses all the others, thereby healing the schizophrenia of categorization." Ligo, *The Concept of Function*, 95.

4. Stuart Hampshire, "Logic and Appreciation," *Art and Philosophy,* ed. W. E. Kennick (New York: St. Martin's Press, 1964), 580.

5. Friedrich Nietzsche, *Beyond Good and Evil,* trans. Walter Kaufman (New York: Vintage Books, 1989), sec. 197–200.

6. Dana Cuff repeatedly observed this in *Architecture: The Story of Practice.* For this book she shadowed the everyday workings of a number of firms and concluded that "placing a high priority on design requires trade-offs in other domains." Dana Cuff, *Architecture: The Story of Practice* (Cambridge, MA: MIT Press, 1991), 69.

    Alan Colquhoun noted, "There is a tendency in criticism to distinguish between utilitarian and moral criteria, on the one hand, and aesthetic criteria, on the other." See his *Essays in Architectural Criticism: Modern Architecture and Historical Change* (Cambridge, MA: MIT Press, 1981), 28.

7. Nietzsche, *Beyond Good and Evil,* sec. 197–200. He stated, "whether it be that indifference and statue coldness against the hot-headed folly of the affects which the Stoics advised and administered; or that laughing-no-more and weeping-no-more of Spinoza, his so naively advocated destruction of the affects through their analysis and vivisection; or that tuning down of the affects to a harmless mean according to which they may be satisfied, the Aristotelianism of morals; even morality as enjoyment of the affects in a deliberate thinness and spiritualization by means of the symbolism of art, say, as music, or as love of God and of man for God's sake . . . this too for the chapter 'Morality as Timidity.'" Nietzsche, *Beyond Good and Evil,* sec. 109–10.

8. "Only a very small part of architecture belongs to art: the sepulchre and the monument. Everything else, everything that serves a purpose, is to be excluded from the realm of art." Adolf Loos, "Architektur," in *Trotzdem, 1900–1930,* in Karsten Harries, *The Ethical Function of Architecture* (Cambridge, MA: MIT Press, 1997), 107.

9. Harries, *The Ethical Function of Architecture,* 4.

10. Mary Devereaux, "Beauty and Evil," in *Aesthetics and Ethics: Essays at the Intersection,* ed. Jerrold Levinson (New York: Cambridge University Press, 1998), 244.

11. Devereaux, "Beauty and Evil," 245.

12. Devereaux, "Beauty and Evil," 246.

13. Stuart Hampshire, for example, makes such a distinction. He wrote, "The two aspects of morality, the universalizing and the particularizing, correspond to two modes of understanding and explaining, one that is characteristic of the natural sciences, and the other that is characteristic of historical and linguistic studies. "*Morality and Conflict* (Cambridge, MA: Harvard University Press, 1983), 3.

14. John Rawls provided a very concise synopsis: "[T]here is a sense in which classical utilitarianism fails to take seriously the distinction between persons. The principle of rational choice for one man is taken as the principle of social choice as well. How does this view come about? It is the consequence, as we can now see, of wanting to give a deductive basis to an ideal observer definition of right, and of presuming that men's natural capacity for sympathy provides the only perspective from which their moral judgments can be brought into agreement. With this background, it is tempting to adopt the approvals of the impartial sympathetic spectator as the standard of justice." "Classical Utilitarianism, Impartiality, and Benevolence," in *A Theory of Justice* (Cambridge, MA: Belknap Press, 1971), 187.
15. These arguments are discussed in greater detail in Samuel Scheffler, *The Rejection of Consequentialism* (Oxford: Clarendon Press, 1982).
16. These are typical rejoinders made by utilitarians whenever anyone objects to the implications of their impartial stance. Whether people really are systematically stripped of their uniqueness or merely on occasion so deprived by consequentialist moralities, whether a coherent moral system more sensitive to the individuality of moral agents can be emplaced; whether critics of consequentialist moralities are simply trying to justify their last lingering traces of egoism: these are topics of spirited debate best left to moral philosophers. These topics are mentioned here only to introduce the idea that other conceptions critical of consequentialism, but still universal in their ambitions, have been proposed.
17. Kant, *Critique of Judgement,* 64.
18. Kant, *Critique of Judgement*, 80.
19. Kant, *Critique of Judgement,* 224.
20. Kant, *Critique of Judgement,* 221.
21. Dieter Henrich, *Aesthetic Judgment and the Moral Image of the World: Studies in Kant* (Palo Alto: Stanford University Press, 1992), 37. Alan Goldman echoes this idea more recently when he states, "It is in the ultimately satisfying exercise of these different mental capacities operating together to appreciate the rich relational properties of artworks that I shall argue the primary value of great works is to be found." Goldman, *Aesthetic Value*, 8.
22. Anthony Savile, *Kantian Aesthetics Pursued* (Edinburgh: Edinburgh University Press, 1993), 164.
23. Kant, *Critique of Judgement*, 213.
24. Kant, *Critique of Judgement*, 222–23.
25. E. H. Gombrich, "Visual Metaphors of Value in Art," in *Meditations on a Hobby Horse*, 16–21. Gombrich wrote, "The Renaissance was confident that

such renunciation could be directed to higher values within the realm of art. This marks the beginning of a thorough process of sophistication that, for good or ill, has divorced the art of Western civilization from a simple appeal to the senses." Gombrich went on to associate the higher values in art with certain emotional states and with certain virtues:

> What strikes us as "vulgar" in art or design does not merely leave us indifferent, it gives us positive displeasure to the point of making us'"feel sick." Our creation of new visual metaphors for the "chaste and pure" finds its necessary counterpart in a strong aversion to such forms as strike us as meretricious and indecent. The very disgust we feel at the "cheap," the "gaudy," the "sloppy," proves our strong emotional involvement. Nor is the nature of this involvement hard to guess. We react as if we resisted seduction, and this is suggested too by the metaphors we use. We speak of a painting as "pretty-pretty," to imply that such primitive gratification as it offers is not for the grown-up mind. We call it "chocolate-boxy" to describe its inartistic invitation to self-indulgence. Everywhere our reaction suggests that we have come to equate such indulgence with other childish gratifications we have learned to control.

Gombrich, "Visual Metaphors," 17, 20.

26. Gombrich, "Visual Metaphors," 24.
27. Gombrich, "Visual Metaphors," 29. Gombrich seems to have seen this as a one-way street, with culture at large as the originator. "The catchwords of value which the critic discerns in the drift of social trends and to which he, in turn, gives currency, ring in the ear of the creative artist and often guide his preferences or impose taboos. It is all the more important for him to be aware that his metaphors *are* metaphors." Gombrich, "Visual Metaphors," 29. This seems to discount the idea that art is not only one of the ends of culture, but one of its constituent elements; as such it is not merely a recipient but an instigator and interpreter of these values which in turn go back out into other facets of culture to mold and transform it in various ways. The ripples across culture eventually run and overlap in every direction. For this reason, I think it appropriate for the architect to ask, not only "what does my admiration for the Guggenheim, et al. say about my ethics?" but also "what does it do to my ethics as well?"
28. See the introduction to Amartya Sen and Bernard Williams, eds., *Utilitarianism and Beyond* (Cambridge, UK: Cambridge University Press, 1982).
29. Bernard Williams, *Ethics and the Limits of Philosophy* (Cambridge, MA: Harvard University Press, 1985), 129.

30. Williams, *Ethics and the Limits of Philosophy*, 200.
31. Thomas Fisher, "A Call for Clarity," in *Architecture* 7 (June 1999): 47. In a related article, Robert Bruegmann noticed a tendency away from any normative judgments about buildings themselves in contemporary criticism. He wrote, "We have moved from a critique of the building to a critique of society as exemplified in the building. . . . Most of the critics . . . are careful to avoid calling a building 'good' or 'bad' but have said rather it is 'interesting' or 'powerful,' or 'important.'" "Utilitas, Firmitas, Venustas and the Vox Populi: A Context for Controversy," in *The Critical Edge: Controversy in Recent American Architecture*, ed. Tod A. Marder (Cambridge, MA: MIT Press, 1985), 23.
32. Elizabeth Anderson, *Value in Ethics and Economics* (Cambridge, MA: Harvard University Press, 1993), 99.
33. Anderson, *Value in Ethics and Economics*, 99.
34. Arnold Isenberg, *The Selected Essays of Arnold Isenberg* (Chicago: University of Chicago Press, 1973), 182–83.

1. For instance, the introduction to the *Uniform Building Code* states, "The purpose of this code is to provide minimum standards to safeguard life or limb, health, property and public welfare by regulating and controlling the design, construction, quality of materials, use and occupancy, location and maintenance of all buildings and structures within this jurisdiction and certain equipment specifically regulated herein." (Whittier, CA: International Congress of Building Officials, 1988), sec. 102.
2. The preface to the *Standard Building Code*, for example, states, "The use of performance-based requirements encourages the use of innovative building designs, materials, and construction systems while at the same time recognizing the merits of the more traditional materials and systems. This concept promotes maximum flexibility in building design and construction as well as assuring a high degree of life safety." (Birmingham, AL: Southern Building Code Congress International, 1999).
3. Peter J. May and Nancy Stark, "Design Professions and Earthquake Policy," in *Earthquake Spectra* 8, no. 1 (February 1992): 121.
4. May and Stark, "Design Professions": 121.
5. The survey occurred in November and December of 1994 and January of 1995. Approximately 70 were mailed a survey form and 24 responded. Although the number of respondents is relatively low, the data generated is from a narrow, targeted group working in seismic structural design on a regular basis, and therefore qualified to make well-informed responses. No determination of correlation to the entire population of structural designers was attempted or is implied.

6. William T. Holmes, Bret Lizundia, Weimin Dong, and Stephen Brinkman, *Seismic Retrofitting Alternatives for San Francisco's Unreinforced Masonry Buildings: Estimates of Construction Cost & Seismic Damage* (San Francisco: Rutherford & Chekene, prepared for the City and County of San Francisco Department of City Planning, 1990), 51–55.

7. R. L. Sharpe, "Acceptable Earthquake Damage or Desired Performance," in *Proceedings of the Tenth World Conference on Earthquake Engineering* (Rotterdam: A. A. Balkema, 1992), 5893.

8. "Ambitious Retrofit Plan for State," *The San Francisco Chronicle*, 9 February 1995.

9. Seismic Safety Commission, *Northridge Earthquake Turning Loss to Gain*, Report no. 95–01 (Sacramento: Seismic Safety Commission, State of California, 1995), xii.

10. VSP Associates, *The Effects of Changing the Uniform Building Code Seismic Zone from Zone 3 to Zone 4 on the Wasatch Front of Utah (Brigham City to Nephi) Final Report* (Sacramento: 1993).

11. From the predicted large earthquake, "The expected level of peak ground acceleration would be in the range of 0.2 to 0.4g or greater." Paula L. Gori and Walter W. Hays, eds., *Assessment of Regional Earthquake Hazards and Risk Along the Wasatch Front, Utah. U. S. Geological Survey Professional Paper* 1500-A-J (Washington, D.C.: Government Printing Office, 1992), 3.

    Robert Smith wrote, "Important features of Utah's geology are the deep, alluvial-filled valleys that parallel the uplifted bedrock of the mountain ranges. The material underlying the valleys and their configuration affects the passage of seismic waves by amplification of the ground displacement as the waves pass from the high velocity bedrock to the lower velocity alluvium. For waves that cross the valleys the ground amplification may be as large as 2 to 6. This effect constitutes an important contribution to earthquake damage, especially in the valleys adjacent to the Wasatch and East Cache faults." "Fundamentals of Earthquake Seismology," *Earthquake Studies in Utah 1850–1978*, ed. Walter J. Arabasz, et al. (Salt Lake City: University of Utah Department of Geology and Geophysics, 1979), 25.

12. Bernard Williams, "Professional Morality and its Dispositions," in *Making Sense of Humanity and Other Philosophical Papers* (Cambridge, UK: Cambridge University Press, 1995), 196.

13. Ethical deliberations slow down the design process, lead to divergence of attitudes among fellow professionals, and cause personal disquietude.

14. Lawrence Kohlberg, *Philosophy of Moral Development* (Essays on Moral Development I) (San Francisco: Harper & Row, 1984), 126–170.

THE ETHICAL ARCHITECT

15. Carol Gilligan, *In a Different Voice: Psychological Theory and Women's Development* (Cambridge, UK: Harvard University Press, 1982).
16. Lawrence Kohlberg, *Philosophy of Moral Development* (Essays on Moral Development I) *Psychology of Moral Development*. Kohlberg thinks that "our stages constitute a hierarchy of cognitive difficulty with lower steps available, but not used by, those at higher stages," 132.
17. John Stuart Mill, for example, wrote of how people complain that there isn't time to do all the "calculating and weighing the effects of any line of conduct on the general happiness." His answer to this objection was to emphasize that the accumulated wisdom of the ages should have provided ample time to develop the prudence necessary for moral action. Perhaps he was not reckoning with the rapid development of technology in the twentieth century when he wrote this. John Stuart Mill, *Utilitarianism and Other Essays* (London: Penguin Books, 1987), 295.

    Hare thought that such problems could be avoided by a two-level approach; intuitive thinking for everyday problems and critical thinking over consequences for the real tough ones. (R. M. Hare, "Ethical Theory and Utilitarianism," in Amartya Sen and Bernard Williams, eds., *Utilitarianism and Beyond* [Cambridge, UK: Cambridge University Press, 1982].) Harsanyi acknowledges, "We will often lack reliable information about other people's manifest preferences and, even more so, about their true preferences. Our interpersonal utility preferences may also be based on insufficient information, etc." Sloughing this off, he goes on, "But the most fundamental source of uncertainty in our moral decisions will always lie in our uncertainty about the future. . . . It seems to me that careful analysis will almost invariably show that the most important source of moral and political disagreements among people of goodwill lies in divergent judgments about future developments and about the future consequences of alternative policies." John Harsanyi, "Morality and the Theory of Rational Behaviour," in Sen and Williams, eds., *Utilitarianism and Beyond*, 61.
18. Samuel Scheffler wrote about the "appearance of irrationality" of side constraints. Such constraints logically "insist that there are occasions when one must not violate an agent-relative constraint even if that is the only way to prevent more widespread violation of the very same constraint by others." *Consequentialism and Its Critics* (New York: Oxford University Press, 1988), 9.

    Related to the problem of casting UMB owners as transgressors, rather than victims, Scheffler notes a "general puzzle about *victim-based* explanations of agent-relative constraints. Any appeal to the victim's possession of some morally significant property seems unable to explain why we may not victimize one person who has that property in order to prevent the victimization of an even larger number of people, each of whom has the very same property. Such appeals simply make all violations of the constraints look equally objectionable, and thus seem to count in favor of allowing, rather than prohibiting, the minimization of total overall violations. They therefore seem to provide no support for agent-relative restrictions (side constraints), whose function is precisely to forbid minimization." Scheffler, ed., *Consequentialism and Its Critics*, 10. The building owners are recast as transgressors, so as to avoid such a moral problem.

19. J. L. Mackie, "Rights, Utility, and Universalization," in *Utility and Rights*, ed. R. G. Frey (Minneapolis: University of Minnesota Press, 1984), 88.

20. R. M. Hare, "Reply to J. L. Mackie," in *Utility and Rights*, ed. R. G. Frey (Minneapolis: University of Minnesota Press, 1984), 118.

21. Philippa Foot, "Utilitarianism and the Virtues," in Scheffler, ed., *Consequentialism and Its Critics*, 224–42.

22. Horst Rittel and Melvin M. Webber, *Dilemmas in a General Theory of Planning* (Berkeley: Institute of Urban and Regional Development, University of California, 1992).

23. Scheffler noted, "it does not for a moment seem paradoxical for the egoist to say that one ought to maximize one's own advantage even if that means that fewer people overall will be able to maximize theirs." He takes exception, however, to Foot's idea that what "is wrong with injustice, lying, and the like would be, roughly, that the disposition to engage in such activities does not contribute to a good life for the agent, and that the disposition not to does. But this, it seems to me, rather glaringly fails to capture our actual sense of what is ordinarily wrong with these things." "Restrictions, Rationality, and the Virtues" in Scheffler, ed., *Consequentialism and its Critics*, 254–55. If, however, one accepts the possibility that one is acting to one's own advantage, but takes responsibility for this by being willing to go to greater lengths to undo damage caused by so acting, for instance, then one can be both consistent and morally motivated.

CHAPTER 6

1. In Philip Langdon, "Asia Bound," *Progressive Architecture* (March 1995): 46.

2. Michael Sorkin, *Variations on a Theme Park* (New York: Hill & Wang, 1992), xii.

3. "Ten Points on an Architecture of Regionalism: A Provisional Polemic," *Center* 3 (1987): 27. See also Kenneth Frampton, "Critical Regionalism: Modern Architecture and Cultural Identity," in *Modern Architecture: A Critical History* (London: Thames and Hudson, 1985).

4. For a discussion of thick and thin concepts, see chapter four.

5. Richard Rorty takes up the philosophical implications of this position in his provocative essay, "Solidarity or Objectivity?" in *Objectivity, Relativism, and Truth*, Philosophical Papers 1 (Cambridge, UK: Cambridge University Press, 1991), 21–34.

   Making the distinction between "us" and "not us" insists on a certain solidarity from the start. It requires a group to share some moral outlook. Adherents to universalist moralities shun this solution because it assumes the likelihood of situations in which not enough is shared for a discussion to be possible. The point here, as in chapter five, is that for universalist moralities such as utilitarianism to even operate there must be some shared institutions and beliefs that cannot be justified by outcome calculations.

6. "A Delicate Balance," *Architecture* (July 1993): 45.

7. Jonas Salk himself assured the public that this is what Kahn had planned all along. See "A Talk With Salk," *Progressive Architecture* 10 (October 1993): 47.

   Stanford Anderson corroborates this fact in his report from the time of the original design. "The approach from the east presents the visitor with the hard and bleak symmetry of the monumental stairs and the (from this view) windowless concrete buildings. . . . [At] La Jolla . . . there is discussion of an administration and reception building at the head of the eastern stairs." "Louis Kahn in the 1960s," in *Louis I. Kahn* (n.p.: n.d.), 301.

   In 1991, John Ellis also reported, "A freehand sketch drawing from Kahn's office at the time indicates a proposed building at this location, with a circular form of axis, split into two wings." "Deferring to Kahn," *Architectural Review* 12 (December 1991): 73.

8. James Stelle reported the sequence of major revisions that occurred at Kahn's instigation, both during design and after construction had begun, in *Salk Institute, Louis I. Kahn* (London: Phaidon Press, 1993), 2–10.

9. Vincent Scully, "Light, Form, and Power: New Work of Louis Kahn," *Architectural Forum* (August 1964): 162–70.

10. Anderson, "Louis Kahn in the 1960s," 301.

11. "Aalto in Italy," *Architectural Review* 3 (March 1979): 140–45.

12. *Progressive Architecture* 4 (April 1995): 15. Indeed, Kahn has been subject of the posthumous construction of another project, the Library for the Graduate Theological Union on the University of California, Berkeley campus, proposed in 1974 and constructed in 1987.

13. Immanuel Kant, *Groundwork of the Metaphysic of Morals*, trans. H. J. Paton (New York: Harper Torchbooks, 1964), 75.

14. Kant, *Groundwork*, 57.

15. Kant, *Groundwork*, 78.

229

16. "Between Beakers and Beatitudes," *Progressive Architecture* 10 (October 1993): 52–53. See also, Jeffry Kieffer, "Criticism: A Reading of Louis Kahn's Salk Institute Laboratories," *A + U* 4 (April 1993): 3–17.

17. Aaron Betsky, "Save the Salk?" *L.A. Architect* 4 (April 1993): 8–9.

18. Betsky, "Save the Salk?" 8–9.

19. Betsky, "Save the Salk?" 8.

20. Robert Venturi and Denise Scott Brown, "Genius Betrayed," *Architecture* 7 (July 1993): 43.

21. Venturi and Scott Brown, "Genius Betrayed," 43.

22. Venturi and Scott Brown, "Genius Betrayed," 43.

23. Venturi and Scott Brown, "Genius Betrayed," 43.

24. Clifford Geertz, "Art as a Cultural System," in *Aesthetics*, ed. Susan Feagin and Patrick Maynard (New York: Oxford University Press, 1997).

25. See chapter three for a discussion of this process.

CHAPTER 7

1. James S. Ackerman, "Style 1960–61," *Distance Points: Essays in Theory and Renaissance Art and Architecture* (Cambridge, MA: MIT Press, 1991), 4. Meyer Shapiro wrote that "style is, above all else, a system of forms with a quality and a meaningful expression through which the personality of the artist and the broad outlook of a group are visible." *Theory and Philosophy of Art: Style, Artist, and Society* (New York: George Braziller, 1994), 51.

2. Prior to the nineteenth century, the most sophisticated attempts to analyze utility were typological—which sort of form best reflected or was most appropriate for which sort of use. See Alberto Perez-Gomez, *Architecture and the Crisis of Modern Science* (Cambridge, MA: MIT Press, 1983).

   In his *An Introduction to the Principles of Morals and Legislation* of 1789, Jeremy Bentham introduced an concept of utility into contemporary thought. Only in the wake of Bentham could it have occurred to Durand to isolate the ornamental from the necessary. In his *Précis des leçons d'architecture données à l'Ecole royale polytechnique*, Durand wrote, "architecture has no other objective than private and public usefulness, the conservation and happiness of individuals, families, and society." (Paris: J.-N.-L. Durand, 1821) vol. 1, 3. See also Sergio Villari, *J.-N.-L. Durand (1760–1834): Art and Science of Architecture* (New York: Rizzoli, 1990).

3. In their writings of the 1920s, Le Corbusier and Pierre Ozenfant expressed preference for forms that were pre-stylistic in light of their perceived ability to be universally understood. These architects wanted to go beyond beauty, into the realm of sensation. Juan Pablo Bonta, *Architecture and Its Interpretation: A Study of Expressive Systems in Architecture* (New York: Rizzoli International, 1979), 33.

4. Aristotle, *Nicomachean Ethics,* trans. Terence Irwin (Indianapolis: Hackett Publishing, 1985). The virtues Aristotle discussed were "courage, temperance, liberality, magnificence, greatness of soul, good temper or gentleness, being agreeable in company, wittiness, and lastly, modesty, which [was] treated not as a virtue, but akin to one." Alasdair MacIntyre, *A Short History of Ethics* (New York: Collier Books, 1966), 68.

5. Alasdair MacIntyre stated this position well when he wrote, "morality is always to some degree tied to the socially local and particular. . . . [T]he aspirations of the morality of modernity freed from all particularity is an illusion." *After Virtue: A Study in Moral Theory* (Notre Dame, Ind.: University of Notre Dame Press, 1981), 126.

6. Stuart Hampshire argued, "morality and conflict are inseparable: conflict between different admirable ways of life and between different defensible moral ideals, conflict of obligations, conflict between essential, but incompatible interests." *Morality and Conflict* (Cambridge, MA: Harvard University Press, 1983), 1. Hampshire is referring specifically to the ethics of Aristotle and Spinoza in this passage, but the author of this work believes it refers equally well to utilitarian and deontological theories. See also the introduction to Amartya Sen and Bernard Williams, eds., *Utilitarianism and Beyond* (Cambridge, UK: Cambridge University Press, 1982).

7. Le Corbusier, *Towards a New Architecture* (1927), trans. Frederich Etchells (New York: Prager Publications, 1970); Sybil Moholy-Nagy, *Native Genius in Anonymous Architecture* (New York: Scholken Books, 1976); Martin Heidegger, "Building, Dwelling, Thinking," in *Poetry, Language, Thought*, trans. Alfred Hofstadter (New York: Harper & Row, 1971).

8. David Watkin, *Morality and Architecture* (Oxford: Clarendon Press, 1977).

9. Denis Diderot, *Diderot on Art,* vol. 1, *The Salon of 1765 and Notes on Painting* (New Haven: Yale University Press, 1995).

"Air Terminal Turns Leaky." *Rome News Tribune*. 15 September 1991.

"Airport Architect Enters Guilty Plea." *Rome News Tribune*. 26 May 1992.

"Airport Repairs on Hold Until Commission Receives Reports."
    Rome News Tribune. 27 September 1991.

ALBERTI, LEON BATTISTA. *On the Art of Building in Ten Books*. Trans.
    Joseph Rykwert. Cambridge, Mass. and London: MIT Press, 1996.

ACKERMAN, JAMES S. *Distance Points: Essays in Theory and Renaissance Art
    and Architecture*. Cambridge, Mass. and London: MIT Press, 1991.

ALEXANDER, CHRISTOPHER and HOWARD DAVIS. "Beyond Humanism." *Journal
    of Architectural Education*, vol. 35 (fall 1981): 18–24.

ALEXANDER, CHRISTOPHER. "Perspectives: Manifesto 1991." *Progressive
    Architecture*, vol. 72 (July 1991): 108–112.

ALLEN, A. "Ethics: The Language of Architecture." *Canadian Architect*, vol. 26
    (July 1981): 25–27.

ALLSOPP, BRUCE. *Art and the Nature of Architecture*. London: Sir Isaac Pitman &
    Sons, Ltd., 1952.

"Ambitious Retrofit Plan for State." *San Francisco Chronicle*. 9 February 1995.

ANDERSON, ELIZABETH. *Value in Ethics and Economics*. Cambridge, Mass.:
    Harvard University Press, 1993.

ANDERSON, STANFORD. "Louis Kahn in the 1960s." In *Louis I. Kahn*. n.p., n.d.

ARENDT, HANNAH. *The Human Condition*. Chicago: University of Chicago Press,
    1958.

ARISTOTLE. *Nichomachean Ethics*. London: J. M. Dent & Sons, Ltd., 1911.

ARROW, KENNETH J. and TIBOR SCITOVSKY, eds. *Readings in Welfare Economics*.
    Nobleton, Oh.: Richard D. Irwin, Inc., 1969.

ARROW, KENNETH J. *Social Choice and Individual Values*. 2d ed. New Haven: Yale
    University Press, 1963.

Benedikt, Michael. "Between Beakers and Beatitudes." *Progressive Architecture*,
    vol. 74 (October 1993): 52–53.

BENNION, F. A. R. *Professional Ethics: The Consultant Ethics and Their Code*.
London: Charles Knight & Co., 1969.

BENTHAM, JEREMY, "An Introduction to the Principles of Morals and Legislation."
1789. *Utilitarianism and Other Essays*. London: Penguin Books, 1987.

BENTON, TIM and CHARLOTTE BENTON, eds. *Form and Function*. London: Crosby
Lockwood Staples, 1975.

BERLIN, ISAIAH. *Concepts and Categories*. London: Hogarth Press, 1978.

BERNSTEIN, M. H. "Ethical Standards for Architects: A Challenge to
Professionalism." *AIA Journal*, vol. 52 (September 1969): 70–73.

BERNSTEIN, RICHARD J., ed. *Habermas and Modernity*. Cambridge, UK: Polity
Press, 1985.

BETSKY, AARON. "Save the Salk?" *L.A. Architect* (April 1993): 8–9.

BLAKE, PETER. *Form Follows Fiasco: Why Modern Architecture Hasn't Worked*.
Boston: Little, Brown & Company, 1977.

BLAU, JUDITH. *Architects and Firms: A Sociological Perspective on Architectural
Practice*. Cambridge, Mass. and London: MIT Press, 1984.

BLOOMER, KENT C. and CHARLES W. MOORE. *Body, Memory and Architecture*.
New Haven: Yale University Press, 1977.

BONTA, JUAN PABLO. *Architecture and its Interpretation: A Study of Expressive
Systems in Architecture*. New York: Rizzoli International, 1979.

BOULLÉE, ETIENNE-LOUIS. "Architecture, Essay on Art." In Helen Rosenau. *Boullée
& Visionary Architecture*. New York: Academy Editions, 1976.

BRAIN, D. "Practical Knowledge and Occupational Control—The
Professionalization of Architecture in the United States." *Sociological Forum*,
vol. 6 (June 1991): 239–268.

BRUEGMANN, ROBERT. "Utilitas, Firmitas, Venustas and the Vox Populi: A Context
for Controversy." In *The Critical Edge: Controversy in Recent American
Architecture,* edited by Tod A. Marder. Cambridge, Mass. and London: MIT
Press, 1985.

233

BUCHANAN, RICHARD. "Branzi's Dilemma: Design in Contemporary Culture." *Design Issues,* vol. 14, no. 1 (spring 1998): 3–20.

BUDD, MALCOLM. *Values of Art: Pictures, Poetry, and Music*. London: Penguin Books, 1995.

CALIFORNIA ARCHITECTS BOARD. *Architects Practice Act with Rules and Regulations 2000*. Sacramento: State of California Department of Consumer Affairs, 2000.

CALLAGHAN, WILLIAM and others, ed. *Selected Essays of Arnold Isenberg.* Chicago: University of Chicago Press, 1973.

CALLAHAN, JOAN C., ed. *Ethical Issues in Professional Life*. New York: Oxford University Press, 1988.

CAMPBELL, ROBERT. "From Playful to Ethical: Architecture of the 1990s." *Design Quarterly*, vol. 153 (fall 1991): 5–8.

CAPELLI, JOHN, PAUL NAPRSTEK, and BRUCE PRESCOTT, eds. *Ethics and Architecture* Vol. 10, *Via*. Philadelphia: University of Pennsylvania Graduate School of Fine Arts, 1990.

CHAMBERS, SIR WILLIAM. *A Treatise on the Decorative Part of Civil Architecture*. 1791. Reprint, New York: Benjamin Blom, Inc. 1968.

CHANG, RUTH, ed. *Incommensurability, Incomparability, and Practical Reason*. Cambridge, Mass.: Harvard University Press. 1997.

"[ ] Charged for Practicing Without License." *Rome News Tribune*. 3 October 1991.

City and County of San Francisco Voter Information Pamphlet. Consolidated Primary Election, 2 June 1998.

CLARKE, ROBERT W. and ROBERT P. LAWRY. *The Power of the Professional Person*. New York: University Press of America, 1988.

COBB, HENRY. N. "Ethics and Architecture." *Harvard Architecture Review,* vol. 8 (1992): 45–49.

COLLINGWOOD, R. G. *The Principles of Art*. New York: Oxford University Press, 1938.

COLLINS, PETER. *Architectural Judgement*. Montreal: McGill-Queens University Press, 1971.

CONRADS, ULRICH. *Programs and Manifestos of 20th-Century Architecture*. Cambridge, Mass. and London: MIT Press, 1975.

CRISP, ROGER and MICHAEL SLOTE, eds. *Virtue Ethics*. Oxford: Oxford University Press, 1997.

CROCE, BENEDETTO. *Guide to Aesthetics*. Indianapolis, Ind.: Hackett Publishing Co., 1965.

CUFF, DANA. *Architecture: The Story of Practice*. Cambridge, Mass. and London: MIT Press, 1991.

———. "The Architecture Profession." In *The Architect's Handbook of Professional Practice*, edited by David Haviland. Washington, D.C.: American Institute of Architects, 1988.

234

CUMMINGS, R. G., D. S. BROOKSHIRE, and W. D. SCHULZE. *Valuing Environmental Goods: An Assessment of the Contigent Valuation Method.* Savage, Md.: Rowman & Allenfield Publishers, Inc., 1986.

DANTO, ARTHUR. *Embodied Meanings.* New York: Farrar Straus Giroux, 1994.

DEPALMA, DAVIS J., and JEANNE M. FOLEY, eds. *Moral Development: Current Theory and Research.* Hillsdale, N.J.: L. Erlbaum Associates, 1975.

DEWEY, JOHN. *Art as Experience.* New York: Minton, Balch & Company, 1934.

DIDEROT, DENIS. *Diderot on Art.* Vol. 1, *The Salon of 1765 and Notes on Painting.* New Haven: Yale University Press, 1995.

DISSANAYAKE, ELLEN. *What is Art For?* Seattle: University of Washington Press, 1988.

"Doss: [ ] Should Foot Terminal Repair Bill." *Rome News Tribune.* 27 May 1992.

DUCASSE, CURT. *The Philosophy of Art.* 1929. New York: Dover Publications. 1966.

DURAND, J.-N.-L. *Précis des leçons d'architecture données à l'Ecole royale polytechnique.* Vol. 1. Paris: J.-N.-L. Durand, 1819.

EATON, MARCIA MUELDER. "Aesthetics: The Mother of Ethics?" *The Journal of Aesthetics and Art Criticism,* vol. 55, no. 4 (fall 1997): 355–364.

EISENMAN, PETER. "The End of the Classical: The End of the Beginning, The End of the End." *Perspecta,* vol. 21 (1984): 154–173.

——. "Post-Functionalism." *Oppositions,* vol. 6 (fall 1976): 1–3.

EISENMAN, PETER and LEON KRIER. "Peter Eisenman versus Leon Krier 'My ideology is Better than Yours.'" *Architectural Design* vol. 59, no. 9–10 (1989): 7–18.

ELLIS, JOHN. "Deferring to Kahn." *Architectural Review,* vol. 191 (December 1991): 71–73.

ERDE, EDMUND L. "A Method of Ethical Decision Making." In *Medical Ethics,* edited by John F. Monagle. Rockville, Md.: Aspen Publishers Inc., 1988.

FENNER, DAVID, ed. *Ethics and the Arts: An Anthology.* New York: Garland Publishing, 1995.

FINDELI, ALAIN. "Ethics, Aesthetics, and Design." *Design Issues* (summer 1994): 49–67.

FISHER, THOMAS. "A Call for Clarity." *Architectural Record,* vol. 187 (July 1999): 47–48.

——. *In the Scheme of Things.* Minneapolis: University of Minnesota Press, 2000.

——. "Who Makes What? (and How We Could All Make More)." *Progressive Architecture,* vol. 76 (December 1995): 49–55.

FLANAGAN, OWEN and AMÉLIE OKSENBERG RORTY, eds. *Identity, Character, and Morality.* Cambridge, Mass. and London: MIT Press, 1990.

FOOT, PHILIPPA. *Virtues and Vices.* Berkeley: University of California Press, 1978.

FRAMPTON, KENNETH. *Modern Architecture, A Critical History*. London: Thames & Hudson, 1980.

FRANKENA, WILLIAM K, In *Perspectives on Morality*, edited by K. E. Goodpaster. Notre Dame, Ind.: University of Notre Dame Press, 1976.

FREY, R. G. ed. *Utility and Rights*. Minneapolis: University of Minnesota Press, 1984.

GEERTZ, CLIFFORD. "Art as a Cultural System." In *Aesthetics*, edited by Susan Feagin and Patrick Maynard. New York: Oxford University Press, 1997.

GHIRARDO, DIANE, ed. *Out of Site: A Social Criticism of Architecture*. Seattle: Bay Press, 1991.

GIEDION, SIGFRIED. *Space, Time and Architecture: The Growth of a New Tradition*. 4th ed. Cambridge, Mass.: Harvard University Press, 1962.

GILLIGAN, CAROL. *In a Different Voice: Psychological Theory and Women's Development*. Cambridge, Mass.: Harvard University Press. 1982.

GOLDMAN, ALAN H. *Aesthetic Value*. Boulder, Colo.: Westview Press, 1995.

GOMBRICH, E. H. "Four Theories of Artistic Expression." In *Gombrich on Art and Psychology*, edited by Richard Woodfield. Manchester, UK: Manchester University Press, 1996.

———. *Meditations on a Hobby Horse and other essays on the theory of art*. 4th ed. London: Phaidon Press, 1984.

GOODMAN, NELSON. *Problems and Projects*. Indianapolis: Bobbs-Merrill, 1972.

GOODY, JOAN, DAVID HANDLIN, MICHAEL PYATOK, HOMER RUSSELL, MACK SCOGIN, BARTHOLEMEW VOORSANGER, and others. "Ethics." *GSD News* (fall 1995).

GOUINLOCK, JAMES, ed. *The Moral Writings of John Dewey*. Amherst, NY: Prometheus Books, 1994.

GREENBERG, CLEMENT. *Art and Culture: Critical Essays*. Boston: Beacon Press. 1961.

GROPIUS, WALTER. *The New Architecture and the Bauhaus*. Boston: Charles T. Branford Company, n.d.

GUESS, RAYMOND. *Morality, Culture, and History: Essays on German Philosophy*. Cambridge, UK: Cambridge University Press, 1999.

GUTMAN, ROBERT. *Architectural Practice: A Critical View*. New York: Princeton Architectural Press, 1988.

HABERMAS, JURGEN. "Justice and Solidarity: On the Discussion Concerning Stage 6." In *The Moral Domain*, edited by Thomas Wren. Cambridge, Mass. and London: MIT Press, 1996.

———. *Postmetaphysical Thinking*. Cambridge, Mass. and London: MIT Press, 1992.

HAGBERG, G. L. *Art as Language: Wittgenstein, Meaning, and Aesthetic Theory*. Ithaca: Cornell University Press, 1995.

HAMPSHIRE, STUART. "Logic and Appreciation." In *Art and Philosophy*, edited by W. E. Kennick. New York: St. Martin's Press, 1964.

——. *Morality and Conflict*. Cambridge, Mass.: Harvard University Press, 1983.

HARDING, CAROL GIBB. "Intention, Contradiction, Dilemmas." In *Moral Dilemmas: Philosophical and Psychological Issues in the Development of Moral Reasoning*, edited by Carol Harding. Chicago: Precedent Publishing, 1985.

HARRIES, KARSTEN. *The Ethical Function of Architecture*. Cambridge, Mass. and London: MIT Press, 1997.

HAYS, K. MICHAEL, ed. *Architecture Theory Since 1968*. Cambridge, Mass. and London: MIT Press, 1998.

HENDERSON, BRIAN. "A Delicate Balance." *Architecture* (July 1993): 45.

HENRICH, DIETER. *Aesthetic Judgment and the Moral Image of the World: Studies in Kant*. Palo Alto: Stanford University Press, 1992.

HEYNEN, HILDE. *Architecture and Modernity*. Cambridge, Mass. and London: MIT Press, 1999.

HICKEY, DAVE. *Air Guitar: Essays on Art & Democracy*. Los Angeles: Art Issues Press, 1997.

HOBBES, THOMAS. *The Leviathan*. 1651. Amherst, NY: Prometheus Books, 1988.

HOFSTADTER, ALBERT. *Truth and Art*. New York: Columbia University Press. 1965.

HOLMES, WILLIAM T., BRET LIZUNDIA, WEIMIN DONG, AND STEPHEN BRINKMAN. *Seismic Retrofitting Alternatives for San Francisco's Unreinforced Masonry Buildings: Estimates of Construction Cost & Seismic Damage*. San Francisco: Rutherford & Chekene, 1990.

HUBBARD, WILLIAM. *Complicity and Conviction: Steps Toward an Architecture of Convention*. Cambridge, Mass. and London: MIT Press, 1980.

HUME, DAVID. "Delicacy of Taste." In *Essays Moral, Political, and Literary*, edited by T. H. Green and T. H. Grose. London: Longmans, Green and Co., 1898.

HUME, DAVID, "Of the Standard of Taste." In *Essays Moral, Political, and Literary*, edited by T. H. Green and T. H. Grose. London: Longmans, Green and Co., 1898.

"In Thoughtful Debate, AIA Rejects Ethics Changes that Would Allow General Contracting." *Architectural Record*, vol. 162 (July 1977).

JACOBS, JANE. *The Death and Life of Great American Cities*. New York: Vintage Books, 1961.

JENCKS, CHARLES. *The Language of Post-Modern Architecture*. New York: Rizzoli International, 1977.

——. "Death for Rebirth." In *Post-Modernism on Trial*, edited by Andreas Papadakis. London: Academy Editions, 1990, 6.

KANT, IMMANUEL. *Groundwork of the Metaphysic of Morals*. 1786. 3rd ed. New York: Harper & Row. 1956.

——. *The Critique of Judgement.* 1790. Trans. James Creed Meredith. Oxford: Clarendon Press, 1952.

KALAY, YEHUDA, ed. *Evaluating and Predicting Design Performance*. New York: John Wiley & Sons, Inc., 1992.

KENNICK, W. E. ed. *Art and Philosophy*. New York: St. Martin's Press, 1964.

KIEFFER, JEFFRY. "Criticism: A Reading of Louis Kahn's Salk Institute Laboratories." *A + U,* vol. 271 (April 1993): 3–17.

KIMBALL, BRUCE A. *The Professionalization of America: The Emergence of the "True Professional Ideal."* Cambridge, UK: Blackwell, 1992.

KIERKEGAARD, SOREN. *Either/Or: A Fragment of Life*. 1843. Edited by Victor Eremita. London: Penguin Books, 1992.

KITARO, NISHIDA. *Art and Morality*. Honolulu: University Press of Hawaii, 1973.

KLASSEN, WINAND. *Architecture, Gods, & Mortals*. Cebu City, Philippines: University of San Carlos, 1994.

KOHLBERG, LAWRENCE. *Philosophy of Moral Development*. Vol. 1, *Essays on Moral Development*. San Francisco: Harper & Row, 1981.

KOHLBERG, LAWRENCE. *Psychology of Moral Development*. Vol. II, *Essays on Moral Development*. San Francisco: Harper & Row, 1984.

KOHLBERG, LAWRENCE and others. "The Return of Stage 6." In *The Moral Domain*, edited by Thomas Wren. Cambridge, Mass. and London: MIT Press, 1996.

KOSTOF, SPIRO. *The Architect: Chapters in the History of the Profession*. New York: Oxford University Press, 1977.

KRIER, LEON and MAURICE CULOT. "The Only Path for Architecture." *Oppositions*, vol. 14 (fall 1978): 39–53.

KRUFT, HANNO-WALTER. *A History of Architectural Theory from Vitruvius to the Present*. New York: Zwimmer/Princeton Architectural Press, 1994.

KULTGEN, JOHN. *Ethics and Professionalism*. Philadelphia: University of Pennsylvania Press, 1988.

LANGDON, PHILIP. "Asia Bound." *Progressive Architecture*, vol. 76 (March 1995): 43–55.

LARSON, MAGALI. *The Rise of Professionalism*. Berkeley: University of California Press, 1977.

LAUGIER, MARC-ANTOINE. *An Essay on Architecture*. 1753. Los Angeles: Hennessey & Ingalls, 1977.

LE CORBUSIER, *Towards A New Architecture*. Trans. Frederich Etchells. New York: Praeger Publishers, 1970.

LEVINSON, JERROLD, ed. *Aesthetics and Ethics: Essays at the Intersection*. New York: Cambridge University Press, 1998.

LIGO, LARRY L. *The Concept of Function in Twentieth-Century Architectural Criticism*. Ann Arbor: UMI Research Press, 1974.

MACINTYRE, ALASDAIR. *After Virtue*. 2d ed. Notre Dame, Ind.: University of Notre Dame Press, 1984.

MACKIE, J. L. *Ethics: Inventing Right and Wrong*. New York: Penguin Books, 1977.

MARCUSE, HERBERT. *Eros and Civilization*. Boston: Beacon Press, 1955.

MASON, H. E. ed. *Moral Dilemmas and Moral Theory*. New York: Oxford University Press, 1996.

MAY, PETER J. and NANCY STARK. "Design Professions and Earthquake Policy." *Earthquake Spectra*, vol. 8, no. 1 (February 1992): 115–132.

MILL, JOHN STUART. "Utilitarianism." 1861–63. *Utilitarianism and Other Essays*. Ed. Alan Ryan. London: Penguin Books, 1987.

MITCHELL, WILLIAM. *Computer-Aided Architectural Design*. New York: Mason/Charter Publishers, 1977.

MOORE, G. E. *Principia Ethica*. 1903. Buffalo, NY: Prometheus Books. 1988.

MOUNT, ERIC, JR. *Professional Ethics in Context*. Louisville, Ky.: Westminster/John Knox Press, 1990.

MUMFORD, LEWIS. *The Role of the Creative Arts in Society*. Manchester, N.H.: University of New Hampshire, 1958.

———. *The Lewis Mumford Reader*. New York: Pantheon Books, 1986.

NAGEL, THOMAS. *The View from Nowhere*. New York: Oxford University Press, 1986.

NIETZSCHE, FRIEDRICH. *Beyond Good and Evil*. 1886. Trans. Walter Kaufman. New York: Vintage Books, 1989.

NISAN, MORDECAI. "Moral Balance: A Model of How People Arrive at Moral Decisions." In *The Moral Domain*, edited by Thomas Wren. Cambridge, Mass. and London: MIT Press, 1996.

NORBERG-SCHULZ, CHRISTIAN. *Intentions in Architecture*. Cambridge. Mass. and London: MIT Press, 1965.

OCKMAN, JOAN. *Architecture Culture, 1943–1968: An Anthology*. New York: Columbia Books on Architecture/Rizzoli International, 1993.

"On AIA's 'Code of Ethics': A Rebuttal from AIA President Schwing." *Architectural Record*, vol. 168 (July 1980): 13.

ORTEGA Y GASSET, JOSÉ. *Phenomenology and Art*. Trans. Philip W. Silver. New York: W. W. Norton & Company, Inc., 1975.

PANOFSKY, ERWIN. *Meaning in the Visual Arts*. 1955. Chicago: University of Chicago Press, 1982.

PAPADAKIS, ANDREASE, ed. "Post-Modernism on Trial." *Architectural Design*, vol. 60 (1990).

PELLETIER, LOUISE and ALBERTO PEREZ-GOMEZ, eds. *Architecture, Ethics, and Technology*. Montreal: McGill-Queen's University Press, 1994.

PELLIGRINO, EDMUND D., ROBERT M. VEATCH, and JOHN P. LANGAN, eds. *Ethics, Trust, and The Professions: Philosophical and Cultural Aspects*. Washington, D.C.: Georgetown University Press, 1991.

239

PEREZ-GOMEZ, ALBERTO. *Architecture and the Crisis of Modern Science*. Cambridge, Mass. and London: MIT Press, 1983.

PEVSNER, SIR NICHOLAS. *The Sources of Modern Architecture and Design*. London: Thames and Hudson Ltd., 1968.

PLATO. *The Republic*. Trans. Henry Desmond Pritchard Lee. Baltimore: Penguin, 1974.

———. *Gorgias*. Trans. T. Irwin. Oxford, UK: Clarendon Press, 1929.

Qualification and Registration of Architects. Law Governing the Practice of Architecture in Georgia and Rules of the Board. Atlanta: Georgia State Board for Examination, 1983.

RADER, MELVIN and BERTRUM JESUP. *Art and Human Values*. Englewood Cliffs, N.J.: Prentice Hall, 1976.

RAWLS, JOHN. *A Theory of Justice*. Cambridge, Mass.: Belknap Press, 1971.

RAZ, JOSEPH. *The Morality of Freedom*. Oxford: Clarendon Press. 1986.

READ, HERBERT. *Art and Society*. 2d ed. London: Faber and Faber, Ltd., 1945.

———. *Icon and Idea*. London: Faber & Faber, Ltd., 1955.

REST, JAMES and DARCIA NARVAEZ, eds. *Moral Development in the Professions*. Hillsdale, N.J.: Lawrence Erlbaum Associates, Publishers, 1994.

REST, JAMES R. "Recent Research on an Objective Test of Moral Judgment: How Important Issues of a Moral Dilemma are Defined." In *Moral Development: Current Theory and Research*, edited by David J. DePalma and Jeanne M. Foley. Hillsdale, N.J.: Lawrence Erlbaum Associates, Publishers, 1975.

RITTEL, HORST W. and MELVIN WEBBER. *Dilemmas in a General Theory of Planning*. Berkeley: Institute of Urban and Regional Planning, University of California, 1972.

RORTY, RICHARD. "Habermas and Lyotard on Postmodernity." In *Harbermas and Modernity*, edited by Richard J. Bernstein. Cambridge, UK: Polity Press, 1985.

RUSKIN, JOHN. *The Seven Lamps of Architecture*. New York: Noonday Press, 1977.

SAFDIE, MOSHE. "Architecture in Search of an Ethic." *Canadian Architect*, vol. 36 (November 1991): 44–45.

SAINT JOHN WILSON, COLIN. *Architectural Reflections*. Boston: Butterfield Architecture, 1992.

"San Francisco's Prop. L." *Forum*. KQED-FM. 19 May 1998.

SANTAYANA. GEORGE. *The Sense of Beauty: Being the Outlines of Aesthetic Theory*. 1896. New York: Modern Library, 1955.

———"The Nature of Beauty." In *Art and Philosophy: Readings in Aesthetics*. New York: St. Martin's Press, 1964.

SAUNDERS, WILLIAM S., ed. *Reflections on Architectural Practices in the Nineties*. New York: Princeton Architectural Press, 1996.

SAVILE, ANTHONY. *Kantian Aesthetics Pursued*. Edinburgh: Edinburgh University
Press, 1993.

——"Architecture, Formalism, and Self." In *Virtue and Taste: Essays on Politics,
Ethics and Aesthetics in Memory of Flint Scheir*, edited by Dudley Knowles
and John Skorupski. Oxford: Blackwell Publishers, 1993.

SCHAPIRO, MEYER. *Theory and Philosophy of Art: Style, Artist, and Society*. New
York: George Braziller, 1994.

SCHEFFLER, SAMUEL. "Liberalism, Associative Duties, and the Boundaries of
Responsibility." Unpublished paper delivered at the John Dewey Memorial
Lectures, University of Vermont, 1994–1995.

——. *The Rejection of Consequentialism*. Rev. ed. Oxford: Clarendon Press,
1994.

——, ed. *Consequentialism and its Critics*. New York: Oxford University Press,
1988.

SCHILPP, PAUL ARTHUR and LEWIS EDWARD HAHN. *The Philosophy of John Dewey*.
3rd ed. La Salole, IL: Open Court, 1989.

SCHWARTING, J. M. "Morality and Reality." *Ethics and Architecture*. Vol. 10, *Via*.
Philadelphia: University of Pennsylvania, 1990.

SCOTT, GEOFFREY. *The Architecture of Humanism: A Study in the History of Taste*.
1914. Garden City, N.J.: Doubleday & Co., 1954.

SCOTT, STANLEY. "Earthquake Engineering: Observations from California's
Experience." *Earthquake Spectra*, vol. 8, no. 1 (February 1992).

SCRUTON, ROGER. *The Aesthetics of Architecture*. Princeton: Princeton University
Press, 1979.

SCULLY, VINCENT. "Light, Form, and Power: New Work of Louis Kahn."
Architectural Forum (August 1964).

Seismic Safety Commission. *Northridge Earthquake Turning Loss to Gain*. Report
no. 95-01. Sacramento: Seismic Safety Commission, State of California,
1995.

SEN, AMARTYA and BERNARD WILLIAMS, eds. *Utilitarianism and Beyond*.
Cambridge, UK: Cambridge University Press, 1982.

SENNETT, RICHARD. *The Conscience of the Eye*. New York: Alfred A. Knopf. 1990.

SHARPE, R. L. "Acceptable Earthquake Damage or Desired Performance."
Proceedings of the Tenth World Conference on Earthquake Engineering. vol.
10. Rotterdam: A. A. Balkema, 1992: 5891–5895.

SILVETTI, JORGE. "The Beauty of Shadows." *Oppositions*, vol. 9 (summer 1977):
43–61.

SMART, J. J. C. and BERNARD WILLIAMS. *Utilitarianism: For and Against*.
Cambridge, UK: Cambridge University Press, 1973.

SORKIN, MICHAEL. *Exquisite Corpse*. London: Verso Publications. 1991.

——. *Variations on a Theme Park*. New York: Hill & Wang, 1992.

STAMPS, ARTHUR E. "Beyond Technology, The Study of Values." *Architecture California*, vol. 7 (December 1985): 34–35.

STOCKER, MICHAEL. *Plural and Conflicting Values*. Oxford: Clarendon Press. 1990.

———. "The Schizophrenia of Modern Ethical Theories." *Journal of Philosophy*, vol. 73 (1976): 453–466.

STOKES, ADRIAN. *The Invitation in Art*. London: Tavistock Publications, 1965.

Standard Building Code. Birmingham, Ala.: Southern Building Code Congress International, 1999.

TAFURI, MANFREDO. *Architecture and Utopia: Design and Capitalist Development*. Cambridge, Mass. and London: MIT Press, 1976.

"A Talk With Salk." *Progressive Architecture*, vol. 74 (October 1993): 47.

"Terminal Designer [   ] Says Building's Problem 'Not Major.'" *Rome News Tribune*. 19 September 1991.

"Terminal Totally Defective." *Rome News Tribune*. 20 September 1991.

TIGERMAN, STANLEY. *Versus: An American Architect's Alternatives*. New York: Rizzoli International, 1982.

TILGHMAN, B. R. *Wittgenstein, Ethics and Aesthetics: The View from Eternity*. Albany: State University of New York Press. 1991.

TILLICH. PAUL. *On Art and Architecture*. New York: Crossroad Publishing Co., 1987.

TIMMERMAN, HARRY, ed. *Design and Decision Support Systems in Architecture*. Boston: Kluwer Academic Publishers, 1993.

Uniform Building Code. Whittier, Calif.: International Congress of Building Officials, 1989.

United States Department of the Interior. *Final General Management Plan Amendment Environmental Impact Statement: Presidio of San Francisco Golden Gate National Recreation Area California*. Denver: United States Department of the Interior, National Park Service, July 1994.

VALLENTYNE, PETER, ed. *Contractarianism and Rational Choice: Essays on David Gauthier's "Morals by Agreement."* New York: Cambridge University Press, 1991.

VENTURI, ROBERT and DENISE SCOTT BROWN. "Genius Betrayed." *Architecture*, vol. 82 (July 1993): 41.

VENTURI, ROBERT. *Complexity and Contradiction in Architecture*. 2d ed. New York: Museum of Modern Art, 1977.

VILLARI, SERGIO. *J.-N.-L. Durand (1760–1834): Art and Science of Architecture*. New York: Rizzoli International, 1990.

VIOLLET-LE-DUC, EUGENE EMMANUEL. *The Lectures on Architecture*. 1875. Trans. Benjamin Bucknall. New York: Dover Publications, 1987.

242

VITRUVIUS. *The Ten Books on Architecture*. Trans. Morris H. Morgan. New York: Dover Publications, 1960.

WATKIN, DAVID. *Morality and Architecture*. Oxford: Clarendon Press, 1977.

WHITE, ANTHONY. *Ethics and Architects in the U.S. and England: A Selected Bibliography*. Monticello, IL: Vance Bibliographies, 1986.

WILENSKY, HAROLD. "The Professionalization of Everyone?" In *The American Journal of Sociology*, vol. 69 (September 1964): 136–158.

WILLIAMS, BERNARD. *Making Sense of Humanity*. Cambridge, UK: Cambridge University Press, 1995.

———. *Moral Luck*. Cambridge, UK: Cambridge University Press, 1981.

———. *Ethics and the Limits of Philosophy*. Cambridge, Mass.: Harvard University Press, 1985.

WITTGENSTEIN, LUDWIG. *Culture and Value*. Edited by G. H. Von Wright. Trans. Peter Winch. Chicago: University of Chicago Press, 1980.

"Woes Mount for Terminal Designer." *Rome News Tribune*. 17 September 1991.

WOTTON, HENRY. *The Elements of Architecture*. 1624. Reprint, Farnborough, UK: Gregg International Publishers Ltd., 1969.

WRIGHT, FRANK LLOYD. *Modern Architecture (The Kahn Lectures 1930)*. Carbondale, Ill.: Southern Illinois University Press, 1931.

ZINK, SIDNEY. "The Moral Effect of Art." In *The Problems of Aesthetics*, edited by Eliseo Vivas and Murray Krieger. New York: Rhinehart & Company, 1958.

Brain, David, 12
Bruegmann, Robert, 225n. 31
Building codes, interpretation of, 129–32, 156
Building performance, 133
Buridan's ass, parable of, 88

C
California Seismic Safety Commission, 143–44.
Chambers, William, 39, 44
Chang, Ruth, 74, 79
Chen, Nelson, 160–61
Classicism, 52–53
Cobb, Henry, 9
Collingwood, R. G., 50
Commoditie. See Utilitas
Complexity and contradiction, 42, 46
Conflict theory, 11–12, 23, 30
Conflicts in design, 65
Consequentialist thinking, 151, 154, 156
Construction czar, 16
Context: as a normative concept, 165–66; as a value, 182–84; historicist approach to, 168–73
Contractarian theory, 10–11, 20, 31, 206
Conventional moral reasoning, 149–50
Covering values, 74–76
Critical regionalism, 163–64
Cuff, Dana, 12

D

E

F

G

W